CHANGING FACE OF TRIPURA TRIBE

CHANGING FACE OF
TRIPURA TRIBE

K.N. Jena
Babu Dhan Tipura

ABHIJEET PUBLICATIONS
DELHI 110094

ABHIJEET PUBLICATIONS
2/46 Tukhmeerpur Extension
Delhi-110094
Phone: 011-22960492, 65698474
E-mail: abhijeetpublication@gmail.com

CHANGING FACE OF TRIPURA TRIBE

First Published 2009

ISBN 978-93-80031-17-0

PRINTED IN INDIA

Published by J.K. Singh for Abhijeet Publications, Delhi-110 094, Lasertypeset by Gaurav Graphics, New Delhi and Printed at Himanshu Printers, Delhi.

Foreword

It is a great pleasure to go through the script titled 'CHANGING FACE OF TRIPURA TRIBE' authored by Dr. K.N. Jena and Sri Babu Dhan Tripura. I am of sincere opinion that the script is an honest attempt to delve deep into the issues and challenges that the Tripura tribe encounters in the era of globalization. This academic exercise is based upon thorough empirical work with credible references. The book reveals interesting aspects of the socio-economic life of Tripura tribe and how it is going through a slow yet steady transition concerning its life style vis-a-vis the process of globalization in North-East India. I hope this book would go a long way in motivating other scholars to embark upon original research work on tribal life in North-East India.

Prof. Rajani Ranjan Jha
Department of Political Science
Benaras Hindu University

Acknowledgements

For completing this volume titled 'CHANGING FACE OF TRIPURA TRIBE' we have received valuable co-operation from a number of people, agencies and organisations. Hence, though we are not in a position to name them but we here by acknowledge that without their co-operation it would not have been possible to bring out this book to the notice of one and all.

Special thanks also due to Moushumi Jena and Mousumi Tripura for their constant moral supports in accomplishing this humble task.

We are also extremely indebted to our colleagues in our respective work places, for their critical inputs and constructive feedbacks in making this book a reality. Our indebtedness to Prof. Arunodoy Saha, Hon'ble Vice-Chancellor, Tripura University, knows no bound, as his constant goading for academic excellence has instilled new impetus among the academic fraternity of Tripura University and we are privileged to be modest stake holders of that constituency.

Dr. K.N. Jena

Sri Babu Dhan Tripura

Contents

Introduction

Study of globalization must precede any attempt to improve the present standard of living of any people, race or tribe. When we speak of 'Tripura Tribe' it is quite unfortunate that there has not been any significant study till today on the life, culture and socio-economic profile on Tripura tribe vis-a-vis impact of globalization in India and North-East in particular. While always speak of tribal welfare, development and upliftment of tribal people. We don't have any comparative study of the tribals in North-East India.

Tripura tribe existed along with its kingdom thousands and thousands of years before the establishment of other tribes inhabited in Tripura. The Tripuras are an important tribe in Tripura. They are the hostess tribe of Tripura. The Tripuras with a population of 2,16,033 was listed wrongly under Tripuri and Noatia community. Since 1961-71 to 2001 Census reports they are enlisted as Tripuri and Noatia. But it was made clear in the survey report of Hill Tipporah in 1874-75 by W.W. Hunter the numbers of Tipperah was 27,148. But Somendra Deb Varma in the Census report of 1931 set the number as 17,098 and termed them Tripuras not as Tripuris or Noatias. However the sudden abolition of Tripura tribe from the list of tribes and their listing with the other communities prompted us to embark upon a scientific reading of Tripura tribe in Tripura.

As no comprehensive study whatsoever on the 'Tripura community' has been conducted and no anthropologist or Sociologist or any other scholars have previously taken up this subject for scientific field-oriented investigation, the primary purpose behind this undertaking has been to make scientific reading and to present a complete picture of the Tripura community in the era of globalization. Such a study would enable the researchers to make further comparative study of culture, socio-economic profile with reference to other nineteen tribes inhabited in Tripura or other tribes of this region.

Apart from academic considerations, the present study has also been undertaken with a pragmatic approach for facilitating policy research. As we know, both the Central and State Government have now seriously undertaken various development projects and welfare measures for the uplift of the tribal peoples. But for a meaningful planning and effective implementation of tribal welfare measures or similar development projects, a scientific policy research and reading of the Tripura tribe of great relevance. This book on the Tripura community, along with focus on the changes brought about by their close contact with the process of globalization and alien cultures, would undoubtedly serve as a perspective for fruitful planning and working out all development and welfare measures.

Lastly, as the Tribal communities of Tripura mostly belong to the same linguistic and ethnic family. The study of the Tripuras would also considerably project a picture of the tribal culture in the state. Again we feel a comprehensive research work on the Tripura Tribe would go a long way in inspiring more and more people to go for intensive researcher work on Tripura tribe as well as other tribes of North-east India.

1

Identity of Tripura Tribe

Derivation and Meaning

The origin and identity of indigenous people inhabited in North-East region are similar to one-another. Reference to these indigenous people in the Vedas, *Ramayana, Vishnu Purana, Kalika Purana, Rajmala,* different scholars of ancient, medieval and modern, personal interview of elders, etc., goes to prove the antiquity of their settlement in the part of North-east India. The Tripuras of the Borok-tribes inhabited in North-East region are belongs to Sino-Tibetan family sub-family of Tibeto-Borok family of Mongoloid origin. The Tripuras were known as Borok and speak their own mother tongue *Korokborok,* (along with other *Korok-Borok* speaking groups). Risley's view on the Mongoloid, "no one who is acquainted with the population of the lower Himalayas can be failed to observe that in the West there has been a substantial intermixture of Indo-Aryan elements, while in the East the prevailing type down to the verge of the plain is exclusively Mongoloid". It is proved with the Risley's point of view that Tripuras along with other inhabitants tribes of north-eastern India belong to Mongoloid origin.

The original homeland of this community is shrouded in mystery. The original homeland of the Tripuras can be identified in the Chung-Ha (Chung-king) south-east of central China near the River Yangtze. Yayati the great king of the lunar dynasty had conquered the seven Islands or lands (Sapta-dvipa) in one round by his chariot. Later on he had divided among his five sons viz. Yadu, Turvasu, Druhyu, Anu, and Puru. The first two sons were by Devayani, daughter of Sukracharya and later three sons were born of Sarmistha, who was a princess. Yadu the eldest son was given to rule over the small kingdom Mathura, Turvasu was made a king of the Yavana Kingdom, and Druhyu became king of the Kirat land, Anu was made king of an eastern country and Puru the youngest son came to be a king of Hastinapura. King Druhya moved extremely towards south-west after crossing Yangtze River near the headwaters of Lohit River and then embraced Brahmaputra River. They moved further down the course of the Brahmaputra and reached in the Nowgaon region. They could not move northward beyond Nowagaon because of strong opposition in the Varman dynasty (C.310-650) which started spreading its influence from Kamrup. So they moved westward, crossed the North Cachar hills and reached plain lands of Cachar. The North Cachar hills stands between two big valleys: the Brahmaputra valley in the east and the Barak Valley in the west. In the Brahmaputra valley where the influence of the varman dynasty was rapidly spreading, the Tripuras did not feel safe, and could not hold their head high. So they drifted westward across the North Cachar hills and then towards south-west reached in the Sagar Island at the mouth of Ganga. They find it as a fertile field, resourceful and evergreen forest, temperate climate and life easy. So, Druhyu the king of the Kirat land, descendent of Tripuras constructed a city in the Trivega region and his capital at the bank of the River Kapila. The boundaries of his kingdom were extended the River Twirong (Brahmaputra) on the North, Arkan on the south, Mekhali

(Manipur) on the east and Koch-Bihar and Vanga or Bangal on the west. It is during the time of King Tripura, by unknown natural calamities that areas was destroyed and as a result the inhabitants of those areas moved to different places. After much suffering Trilocan the son of king Tripura rebuilt the new land Tripura and its race Tripuras which was bear to his father's name. The present boundary of Tripura kingdom lies bounded by Bangladesh on the West, the North-West, the South and the South-East territory while Assam and Mizoram bounded it on the North and the East respectively.

The Genesis

The great migration? After centuries of fragmentation and feuds, china was unified for the first time under the Sue dynasty (589-618 A.D.). So they left china long before Sue dynasty ascended the throne. Buddhism was introduced in China in 65 A.D. At the time of their immigration they were animists. So it may be reasonably assumed that they emigrated before 65 A.D.

What is meant by Kirata? Who were Kiratas? The Kirata has been explained by R.M. Nath in his book, The back ground of Assamese culture, as follows : "The word silk is derived from the original Mongoloid-sirkek, Korean-sir, Chinese-ssi, Greek-ser, Latin-sericum. The word sari, wearing cloth of Indian ladies, is derived from ser. The dealers in silk were called the seers or the scyrites. The word Scyritae, Cirrhadae and karate appears to have had originally referred to dealers in silk. Silk was originally produced in china and it was catered by merchants of Turkestan through Tibetan intermediaries to India and Assam. That there was an ancient route from China along the course of the Lohit River to Assam has already been mentioned. The Zuh-this people came to Assam valley by this route. The Chinese record of about 248 A.D. mentions a trade route from Yunan in South China through Shan states, Hukuong valley, the

Brahmaputra River, and Kamrupa to Patliputra (patna) and Sravasti. In ancient times traders from different parts of Tibet, Central Asia and China flocked to Tripura kingdom, present North-east India through various routes, and as they traded mostly in silk, they were generally called Seers-Cirrahadoi-Syrites-Cirata-Kirate".

The Tripura on march: After long years in the house of 39th king Daitya from Druhyu, a son was born. The king named his son Tripura, because of his born in the Trivega country. After his father's death he became a king of Kirat land in his father throne. The king Tripura, whose domain was most of the North-East India, had changed KIRATA land into TRIPURA in his name and his race became to be known Tripura.

The term 'Tippra or Tripura' originated from its first capital of Tripura kingdom of Tribeg at Sagar Island, where 24 nos. kings ruled there from Druhya to Pratardhan. It was coined meaningfully corresponding to the nature, geography and landscape of the place where Ganga, Brahmaputra and Meghna meet. It has beautiful places having the landscape in the valleys adjoining to foothills availing themselves the advantages of important river. This had been lost possibly on account of Tsunami and earthquake.

The word 'Tripura' is combination of three Korokborok terms namely, Tui+Bu+Pra which 'Tui' means Water; 'Bu' (Bupra) denotes adjoining Rivers and Streams of the Region and 'Pra' means Village. It is Borok village or inhabited near the water, adjoining Rivers and streams of the region became known as Tripura.

Now, what does the term Tribe/Tribal mean. The term 'Tribe' in *korokborok* is 'Dopha'. Tribe/Tribal were first introduced by the British colonial Administration and foreign anthropologists. According to the understanding of those Colonial Administrators the people so called Tribe/Tribal in their sense is semi-Hinduised. In the course of the 20th century, the use of TRIBAL word is generally to narrow down to the people belonging to particular race, who are still referred to as TRIBAL. The Britishers and Bengali scholars who could not pronounce properly of korokborok terms even changed the name of Tripura Kingdom and its race as 'TIPPERAH'or Tiphras or Deshi and Puran Tripura, etc.

Many scholars have given their views about the identity of Tripura and her race. These are:

According to *Rajmala,* Tripura Tribe whoever, have taken the status of Kshatriyas, claim descendants of the lunar Race. Twelve sons were born in the house of King Trilochana, viz. Drikpati, Dakshina, Daksha, Dhrumayu, Dhrabin, Dhristhyghnya, Bhrigu, Dhurdhar, Dhruha, Dhushmayu, Doubiry and Dhamna. They came to be known as twelve Tripura families. They belong to the Royal House of Tripura and are installed as a king, if need be. None else are entitled to the Royal umbrella in the Tripura state. If, it so happens at any time that no son is born to a king, then any relation or kith of king of this twelve families can be made king. The children born in these twelve families are called Tripura, people of Royal descent. Tripura is people by the – Tripuras". Thus was how Tripura Tribe came to exist. (Sri Rajmala by Dr. N.C. Nath, p. 27).

In the same vein the *Rajmala* gives a similar account but slightly differ in the flows of the history. It says by D. P. Debbarma, "King Druhya, the youngest son of Jajati of lunar dynasty married a Bodo Princess for which he was disinherited. He therefore, established a new dynasty in the North Eastern India defeating the kings Kirates. His Progeny become the ruling race. Then Pratardon, the 26th descendants from Druhya came over to Assam and founded a kingdom named TRIVEGA in about 1900 BC with his headquarters at the bank of the river Kapila in the present Nowgong district.

The dynasty ruled here for full fourteen generations. Then Daitya, the 13th descendants from Pratardon ascended the throne and enlarged the kingdom. And Tripur, the son of Daitya was unpopular for his arrogance nature and administration. He was disliked by his people and for which they say that he was assassinated by God Shiva. On his death, who's named still bears as TRILOCHAN, the son of Tripur became the king and married the daughter of the neighboring Kachari king of Heramba, was how the story goes".

During 1430-31 A.D., Dharma the eldest son of the king Maha Manikya, turned a monk, as a result of his past deeds, and went away visiting different places. During his visit to Vanauaci, he fell asleep beneath a tree. A Brahman from Kanuj, Kautuka by name, living at Varanasi together with his wife saw a Snake with hood expanded over the Monk's head, he hurriedly awakened the Monk lying by the road-side. The Brahman asked him 'What country do you belong to and why do you undergo so much suffering by residing here?' The Monk replied, "I am a Tripura by race. My kingdom is in the south-east corner and at great distance from here." (Dr. N.C. Nath, Sri Rajmala, Vol. II, p. 57).

Another view, The Tipperah or Tripura originally belong to the stock of Tibeto-Burma and are said to have first settled in a place near present Allahabad. They preferred to call themselves the 'Children of water Goddess' and were therefore known as the Tippra. Latter time they were known as the Tipperah or Tripura. The word Tripura or Tippra is combination of two Korok-Borok terms 'Twi' and 'Pra', which means Water and Village respectively. In another words inhabitant of nearby river-water came to be known as Tripura.

According to R.M. Nath (1948), Tipperah people preferred to call themselves the children of water-goddess and were, therefore known as the Tiphras or the Tippras; and later on they become known as the Tipperahs. Some other believes that the word 'Tripura' has been Sanskritised which originated from 'Tipra'. Tripura derived from 'Tripuram' meaning a "land of three cities or three filled-up substances". Again some believe that a Mythical king Tripur had named his kingdom 'Tripura' after his own name and his clans as Tripura.

According to Kailas Chandra Sinha, the name of Tripura was formed from the Tippra word. In Tripura dialects, 'Twi' means Water and 'pra or Phra' means God. And from Tiphra the people have known as Tiphra.

"The Tipperah Tribes" said captain Lewin, "recognize no generic term by which their race may be distinguished. If you ask a man of what race he is, he will tell you the name of his clan, Purron, Ouie or whatever it may be, but if he speaking a Bengali, he will be use the generic term Tipperah".

Another view is that, "Tripura is the land of the God Siva who is also known as Tripuresha. The people who settled in the land of Tripuresha Siva came to be known as Tripura Tribe and the land as Tripura".

Dr. Suniti Kumar Chatterjee classified the Tripura Tribe under the Indo-Mongoloids or Kiratas. Linguistically the Tripura Tribe is Bodos. The Bodos, who spread over the whole of the Brahmaputra valley and North Bengal as well as East Bengal, forming a solid block in North Eastern India, were the most important Indo-Mongoloid people in eastern India and they form one of the main bases of the present day population of those tracts. Judging from the wide range of extension of their language, the Bodos appear first to have settled over the entire Brahmaputra valley, and extended to west into North Bengal (in Koch Bihar, Rangpur and Dinajpur district). They might have pushed into North Bihar also and the Indo-Mongoloids who penetrated into North Bihar might equally have been either Bodos or 'Himalayan' tribes allied to the Newars. They skirted the southern bend of the Brahmaputra and occupied the Garo Hills, where as Garos they form a block of Bodo speech. South of the Garo Hills they spread in Northern Mymensingh, where the semi Bengali Hajong is of Bodo origin. From Nowgong district in Assam their area of occupation extended to Cachar district (particularly in the North Cachar Hills) and into Sylhet, and they moved further to the South, to Tripura state, where there is still a Bodo-speaker block in the shape of the Tipra tribe which bounded the state, and from Tripura they spread into Comilla and possibly also to Noakhali district, and thus they occupied the mouth of the Ganges by the eastern sea".

According to Dr. B.K. Burua, "the original home of these speakers, were western china near the Yang-Tse-Kiang and the Hwang-ho rivers. From there they went down the course of the Brahamaputra and the Chindwin and the Irrawady and entered India and Burma. The swarm which came to Assam proceeded down to the great bend of the river Brahmaputra near Dhubri. From there, some of them went to the south and occupied first the Garo hills and the state of Hill Tippera".

According to Hunter "The rulers of Tripura were Tibeto-Borok in origin". Hunter (1876) further remarks that the name 'Tripura' was given in honour of the Temple at Udaipur. This Temple now ranks as the second Tirtha place; it was dedicated either to Tripurdhana, the Sun God or to Tripureswari, the mistress of the "three ward", (heaven, Earth and Hell). It is believed that the name 'Tripura' has been derived from Tripurasundari, the main deity of the land. Major Fisher has opined that "the Tipperas and the cacharis are of the same origin and their customs, religion, appearance are also probably same". In *Rajmala* also it is mentioned that " there was connection between the Tripuras and the Cacharis". Sidney Endly says that "in feature and general appearance they approximate very closely to the Mongolian type, and this would seem to point to Tibet and China as the original home of the race".

In Alexander Mackenzie's book it is written that "the

inhabitants were of two very distinct classes, one of which, doubtless, originally came from China, but was now of the Hindoo persuasion; the other, a people call KooKies or Coocis". (*The North East Frontier of India,* A. Mackenzie, Reprint 1979/p. 275).

He further says that, "there would seem to be good reason for believing that the Kachari (Bada) race is a much more widely distributed one than it was at one time supposed to be. They are undoubtedly found well outside the limits modern (political) Assam, i.e. in North East Bengal Koch-Bihar, and also in Hill Tippera where the language of the people gives decisive evidence that they are of the Bada stock".

The Bodos who live in Tripura near the Southern boundary of Assam are known as Tripuras. It is assumed that according to the name of Tripura state, they are named Tripuras.

Besides these, it is acknowledged that in early periods of Tripura dynasty there was marital relation between the Royal families of Tripura and Bodo. The Tripura king also established his kingdom in Kiratadesh by defeating the Kirata king, Kiratadesh is at present under the province of Assam.

Beyond above cited views of different scholars of the origin of Tripura Tribe, during my interviews with older generation of Tripura tribe, it has been noticed that they introduced themselves as Tipra in present form Tripura. They have their own identity and unique culture. They have demand deadly as a Tripura Tribe son of king Tripura from the descendent of king Yayati of lunar dynasty.

In conclusion, however, there are certain areas to which intentionally or unintentionally avoid to use as a ruler for digging out the reality of the royal history of Tripura. And it is applicable to any other people groups of this world if one is to find out the correct history of the concerned people. It is simple but natural which man can undo or composed out of human erudition. This is the true rod to measure, the right scale to weight, the correct spectacle to see, and the genuine hypothesis to prove the unsolved mystery. It is none other than the appearance, mentality, personality, world-views, religion, body structures and so forth that define and confirmed who is who. With that sort of estimation, the descendents of the king Maharaj Tripura and Rajas of Tripura are the present Tripuras and Mongoloid by race, is without question. Some orthodox scholars may out of personal gratification, would like to forcefully bridge the Tripura royal tribe with Kshatriya of the lunar dynasty. But the truth is that, in no way one can say that Mongoloid and the Aryans are same blood. It is like saying black and white is same colour. Therefore, the royal dynasty of Tripura from which the Tripuras belonged is Sino-Tibetan family sub-family of Tibeto-Borok family of Mongoloid origin. Who are socially, culturally, linguistically influenced by the Hindus.

Regarding the identity of Tripura Tribe, many scholars and authors have given similar and contradictory opinions. However it is assumed that the Tring, Tipperah, Tiphra, Tipperas and Tippras written or used by different researchers are corrupted form of present Tripura Tribe. To an outsider's observations there is nothing more confusing and complicated than the surname or title of the Tripura.

Clans of Tripuras

Being the Royal Tribe of the kingdom, the Tripura tribe was once divided into different groups based on their respective presentations. The king led them to categorize themselves into different sections according to their presentations which later made them as clan, as any other tribes had. Generally the Tripura Tribe clans are named after a particular leader or a heroic deeds, profession, bank of rivers and places or village to which the group originally belonged and resided. The dopha or Clan of Tripura Tribe are divided into 21(twenty-one) groups. They are—ANOK, KEOA, NAITONG, KHAKLUK, PHATUNG, MONGBAI, TONGBAI, KHALI, GAIBENG, HARBANG, DENDOK, ASLONG, MORBENG, HAPANG, TOIMUKDOK, TOTARAM, BILOK, GAIGRA, GWRJWNG, LIGA AND SAKA RUPINI. These clans descended from twelve Tripura families. Twelve Tripura families were known from twelve sons born in the house of Trilocan. Trilocan was born in the womb of Hirabati, wife of Tripura after his death. Tripura is a son of Daitya, descendent of Druhya.

According to *Rajmala,* 'Twelve sons were born in the house of Trilocan. They came to be known as the Twelve Tripura families (Nokhung-Chinwi Tripura). They belong to the royal house of Tripura and entitled to be installed as a king, if need be. None else are entitled to the royal umbrella in the Tripura state. If it so happens at any time that no son is born to a king, then any relation or kith and kin of these twelve families can be made king. The children born in the twelve families are called Tripura people of royal descent. *(Raj vamsi Tripura)*

In the reign of Maharaj Bir Chandra manikya (1862-96) these clans had been divided into five groups as 'Pancha-Tripura' namely: Tripuras, Reangs Tripura, Jamatwiyas Tripura, Noatias Tripura, and Halams Tripura. He introduced Pancha-Tripura for the better and efficiency functioning of the administration.

In the nineteen century The Tripuras had been sub-divided as Old Tripuras and Deshi Tripuras, Reangs, Jamatias, Noatias and Halam. S.B.K. Dev Varma in his book, *'The Tribes of Tripura: A Dissertation'*, mentioned, "The Tripura along with Deshi Tripuras, the Jamatias, the Noatias and the Reangs are commonly known as 'Kshatriya'".

According to *Rajmala* and modern scholars, the Reangs, the Debbarmas, the Jamatias, the Noatias and Kolois and Rupini of Halams belongs to Tripura clans.

For the sake of information, brief backgrounds of some clans are highlighted below:

ANOK: The word 'Anok' is coined from two *Korokborok* terms 'ANI' and 'NOK', which 'Ani' means 'My' and 'Nok' means 'Hut'. In another way it means 'My land'. A King of Triveg once built a beautiful and unique hut which anyone seeing it, were bound to ask whose hut is it. The owner would just stand by his hut and say, 'Ani Nok' meaning 'My Hut'.

He and his reply (Ani Nok) for his hut became so popular that people know him as Anok. After his death, his race was known as 'Anok' after his popular name. This clan constitutes the major population among Tripuras in Tripura and Bangladesh.

Naitong : The Naitong clan of Tripura Tribe is purely combination of two Korokborok words that is 'NAI' and 'TONGNAI', which 'Nai' means 'observe' and 'Tongnai' means 'Guard'.

Khakuluk : The term Khakuluk literally means White Gourd. There is a legendary regarding this particular clan Khakuluk. Once in a social gathering of Pomang, white gourd is cooked with Pork and served in the gathering due to shortage of pork towards the end. People who came in that gathering and had food criticized the pomang for being so mean and serving pork mixed with khakuluk. Since then, his descendants were known as Khakuluk.

Mongbai: The term Mongbai is a combination of two Korok borok words 'Mong' and 'Kabai'. 'Mong' means barn where paddy is stored. 'Kabai' means break. Mong + Kabai= Mongbai. This clan is the descendant of a family whose barn was broken due to storage of huge amount of paddy which is beyond the capacity of the barn. Since then this particular family and its descendants are recognized clan as Mongbai.

Tongbai: Tongbai is a fusion of two word; Tong and Kabai. (Tong + Kabai = Tongbai) Tong means paddy measuring container (One Tong equals to a measure of 10 Kg. paddy). Kabai means break.

Keua: The term 'Keua' is coined from two words— 'Ker' and 'Ua'. Ker comes from the word para Kermani which is a ritual performed by the Tripuras, where the particular village is bounded by some mantras and a gate placed in the entrance of the village. The gate is made of bamboo called 'ua' the bamboo is carved and decorated beautifully. Since that bamboo is used in those rituals, the word Kewa is termed from Para Kermani ua.

Clans are sub-divided into 'sandai'. The *korokborok* term *Sandai* literally means lineage. The Tripura Tribe Sandai is named after some animals, birds, bamboos, waterfalls, etc as most of the groups and sub-groups of the Kokborok speaking tribals of Tripura had. The Tripuras' lineages are patriarchal. The members of the different lineages are known according to their respective ancestors. As the members of a lineage are related, their behavioural character is also similar to certain extent.

The Sandai of Anok are as follows:

1. Dwising.	2. Muichang.	3. Duwari.
4. Kongdai.	5. Kasin.	6. Kerang.
7. Nakang.	8. Hachuk.	9. Guld.
10 Dogrong.	11. Dong-gro.	12. Kailangsi.
13. Langta.	14. Duwinesa.	15. Khaima.
16. Harbang.	17. Ramasa Hajara.	18. Atharo Hajara
19. Sharba Yakbai.	20. Dana Hajara and	21. Ramasa Uanjoy.

The Sandai again divided as Desw into five groups. They are—

1. Baklap Desw,
2. Bokrong Desw,
3. Ramwk Desw,
4. Kuchuk Desw and
5. Guld Desw.

The Desw performs enrich rules and regulations during the marriage ceremonial. Whenever there are inter-marriages between two Desw, there will be a demand from the youth of particular bride Desw.

In conclusion, this grouping was based on works, representations, language, cultural and socio-economic factors. This does not mean that they were totally different from one another. It seemed to be a matter of slight differences. Besides, it also was perhaps a consequence of geographical differentiation or isolations to one another. These days we can not see so much fashion on it.

From the above chart we can see the origin of Tripuras. It is very clear that the origin is at China in the plain of Chung-ha near the Yangtze River and South to the Hwangho River. From there, they crossed over the Yangtze River towards the west and entered the North-east India through Lohit River and reached the Barak valley. From Barak valley they moved towards extreme south and reached an island in the mouth of the river Ganga and Brahmaputra. They formed a city in that island and named it Triveg. At present it is known as the sunderbans which lies in West Bengal and Bangladesh. Due to unknown natural calamities that area was destroyed and as a result the inhabitants of that areas moved to different places. Some of the Tripuras, who are thought to be developed, changed their community and titles in to new ones as seen on the above chart on the right side. They are Tripuri (Tripuras and Debbarmas), Reang, Jamatia, Uchoi, Koloi, Rupini, Murasing and Noatia. The list of

Chart 1: Origin of Tripura Tribe:

SINO-TIBETAN

- Chinese
- Thai
- Tibeto-Borok
  - Bodo
  - Dimasa
  - Garo
  - Hojong
  - **Tripura**
  - Kuch
  - Mech
  - Rabh
  - Tiwa
- Tibeto-Burma

Tripuras

1. **ANOK,**
2. **KEOA,**
3. **NAITONG,**
4. **KHAKLUK,**
5. **PHATUNG,**
6. **MONGBAI,**
7. **TONGBAI,**
8. **KHALI,**
9. **GAIBENG,**
10. **HARBANG,**
11. **DENDOK,**
12. **ASLONG,**
13. **GWRJWNG,**
14. **LIGA,**
15. **BILOK,**
16. **KEMA**
17. **TOTARAM,**
18. **SAKA RUPINI,**
19. **HAPANG,**
20. **TWIMUKDOK,**
21. **MARBENG**

Tripuras recognized as separate Tribes.

1. **Noatia**
2. **Tripuris(Gurpai & Tripuras)**
3. **Jamatia**
4. **Reang (Bru)**
5. **Murashing**
6. **Koloi**
7. **Rupini**
8. **Uchai**

tribes as seen on the above chart on the left side are the original Tripuras which are classified under Noatia and Tripuri but still write Tripura and need to be recognized as Tripura community. Instead of recognizing them as Tripuri or Noatia, they should have been recognized as Tripura community. Their recognition is held back as they are under developed and the main responsibility lies with the government and other organizations of the community.

Numerical Strength

According to the Census Report of 2001 total population of Tribals are 9, 86,328. As per Census Reports there are 19 scheduled tribes inhabited in Tripura. There is another one of the major populated tribe known as 'Tripura'. The Tripura Tribe in all the census reports since 1961-71 was wrongly listed as Tripuri community and some with Noatia community. The Tripuris (Tripura and Debbarma) according to Census Report of 2001 is 5,43,848 and Noatias (Tripura and Noatia) is 6,655. There is Tripura tribe since time immemorial in Tripura. To be clarified we may refer Table-3 & 4 below, the survey report of Hill Tipporah of 1874-75 by W.W. Hunter, Tipperah 27,148 and Somendra Deb Varma in his Census report of 1931, mentioned the population of Tripuras as 79,074. However in the present study, we have found that the numerical strength of Tripura tribe in Tripura is 2,16,033 approximately. Now, Tripura community may be listed a separate community in all census based on their unique cultural identity and numerical strength. It is assumed that their population would not be less than other nineteen tribes. It seemed that the Tripura Tribe numerically, may be listed as one of the major tribe among the inhabited tribes of Tripura. Table 5 below may be referred.

Unfortunately, the Tripura tribe is recorded as Tripuris in the Government records instead of Tripura community. But it is interesting to note that the Tripuri community never treated Tripura Tribe as a part of their communities instead they treated as Noatia. The Tripuras of course regard themselves as a separate Tribe, not Tripuri or Noatia. Tripuri (Debbarma) is a pure newly adopted title, since early 1904 A.D. by the SANAD granted by the Governor General of India to the then Maharaj king Radhakishore Manikya period. Before the SANAD they belong to Tripura community known as 'Gurpai' as other Kokborok speaking Tribes in Tripura. Now the question of Noatia which literally means NEW, they are also part of Tripura community, but they are admixture of korokborok speaking peoples. Now, they have their own art and culture.

Who were Tripuris? Tripuris were those people who originated from the twelve Tripura families of Trilocan's twelve sons. Generally, above mentioned twenty-one clans of Tripuras and other korok-borok speaking people are known as Tripuris. Tripuris means not Gurpais or Tripuras or any other major clans of korokborok speaking tribes of Tripura. Tripuris referred to those korokborok speaking people of twelve Tripura families of the Trilocan sons. This is counted at present as twenty-one clans as Tripura community and others as Reangs, Jamatias, Noatias, Kolois, Murasingh, Uchois, Rupinis and Debbarmas.

Tripura Tribe inhibits Amarpur, Sabroom, Santir Bazar, Belonia, Udaipur, Sunamura, Lontrai valley, Gandha chara, Kamalpur, Ambassa, Kailashar, Dharmanagar, Kanchanpur, Sadar, and in some parts of Bishalgarh, Teliamura and Khowai sub-division of Tripura. Tripura tribe also inhibits Hailakandi of Assam, Chittagong and some other parts of East Pakistan at present known as Bangladesh.

Table 3: Tribe wise population of Hill Tipperah in 1874-75 by W.W.Hunter

Tipperah	*Jamatiayas*	*Nowattias*	*Riangs*	*Halams*
27,148	3,000	2,144	2,435	5,577

Table 4: Sub-Division wise population of Tripura Tribe in 1931 as per Somendra Deb Varma.

Sl. No.	*Name of Sub-Division*	*Old Tripura*	*Deshi Tripura*
1.	Agartala	1,780	245
2.	Sadar	41,048	964
3.	Sunamura	3,459	118
4.	Sabroom	933	—
5.	Khowai	20,447	—
6.	Udaipur	690	143
7.	Amarpur	170	15
8.	Kailashar	8165	2
9	Dharmanagar	845	—
10.	Belonia	43	8
	Total	77,580	1,494

Table 5: Sub-Division wise population of Tripura community in Tripura, 2008

Sl. No.	*Name of Sub-Division*	*2008*
South District		
1.	Sabroom	52,644
2.	Belonia	18,761
3.	Santir Bazar	21,869
4.	Amarpur	25,105
5.	Udaipur	5,375
Dhalai District		
6.	Longtrai Valley	43,213
7.	Gandha chara	20,834

8.	Ambassa	5,148
9.	Kamalpur	1070
West District		
10.	Sunamura	12,311
11.	Sadar	1,880
12.	Khowai	192
13.	Bishalgarh	49
14.	Teliamura	221
North District		
15.	Kanchanpur	4,535
16.	Dharma Nagar	1,710
17.	Kailashahar	1,116
	TOTAL	**2,16,033**

Sources: Above mentioned numerical strength was collected from different tribal supervisors, panchayet officers and secretaries, panchayet chairmans and members, Ruwajas and leaders of Tripura Chubalai Buthu.

Language of the Tripura Tribe

Oliver Wendell Holmes said referring to language, "Language is a solemn thing, it grows out of life, out of its agonies, and its ecstasies, its wants and its weariness. Every language is a temple in which the soul of those who speak it is enshrined". The enshrined language spoken by TRIPURAS is called 'KOROKBOROK'. It is the original version of the Tripuras. The term korokborok was coined from two terms- Korok (meaning Language) and Borok (meaning Human Being). This literally means, 'Language of Man' or 'Language of Human'. Practically the language Korokborok is the mother tongue of Tripuras. However, with the development in language with the passage of time and for faster communication, some of the *korokborok* speaking tribes namely Jamatias, Noatias,

Murasings, Debbarmas, Kolois, Rupinis, Reangs, and Uchois adopted the shortened version. The shortened version of *korokborok* like *kokborok* is used by Debbarmas, Murashing and Jamatias and Rupinis, Reangs, Uchois and Kolois uses the word *Kaubru*. The original Tripuras still uses the original term korokborok. Despite there may occur some dialectical differences in tunes and stressing. The first five communities ethnically belong to same group i.e. Tripura, Jamatias, Noatias, Murasings, and Debbarma of Tripura community and ethnically latter four groups do not belong. Among them kolois and Rupinis community ethnically belong to Halam tribe and Reangs and Uchois belong to admixture of Kuki tribe. The non-Tripura groups of the people adopted Tripura language due to century old association with the Tripura people the dominant ethnic group of the state who are claimed to be the original residents of Tripura. Korokborok belongs to the great Sino-Tibetan to Tibeto-Borok linguistic family and it is quite akin to the Bodo language. Unfortunately, korokborok did not survive with written script. At present the Roman script is officially used. Korokborok is one of the major languages among the tribals of Tripura. The language is very rich in every aspect of terminologies.

Language as per the Constitution of India under Article 29(1) states that "any section of the citizens residing in India or any part there of having a distinct language script or culture of its own shall have the right to conserve the same". Article 350A of the Constitution also lays great emphasis on instruction in the mother tongue. In 1951 UNESCO convened an emergency meeting of experts on education. This historical meeting ended with two important suggestions. One is the use of vernacular languages in education and the other the best medium of Teaching is the mother tongue. Article 350A of the Constitution also strongly recommends mother tongue in primary education and called upon the local authorities to create an educational environment where schooling in mother tongue is ensured.

According to Dr. Suniti Kumar Chatterjee, 'The origin and Development of the Bengali language', "The Bodo section of the Tibeto-Burman branch of the Tibeto-Chinese people (Bodo, Mec, Kachari, Rabha, Garo, Tripura) came to Assam and East Bengal, and were spread all over East and North Bengal. The time of Tibeto-Burman incursion and settlement in Assam and East Bengal is not known, but it could not have been long before the beginning of the Christian era, at the earliest". He further noticed, Tripura is akin to old Bodo language. He says, "Nearly 303,030 people in the state have still kept up their old Bodo language, the Tripura or Mrung." (Magnamopous, 1950)

Sir George Abraham Grierson has mentioned Korokborok as TRIPURA in his great book linguistic survey of India. Where he says, "The Bara group, Then comprises the languages spoken by the other tribes shown in the following table.

True Bara (Kachari and Mech)

Rabha

Lalung

Dima-Sa (Hills Kachari)

Garo

Tripura and

Chutiya- to this list must be added one more name Moran. This was the language of a Tribe now completely hinduised in Sibsagar and Lakhimpur.

According to Warren W. Smith, "the Ch'iang and Tibeto-Burman languages are generally thought to be related". According to Pulleyblank and Gordon Bowles, 'the language of modern Ch'iang is classified as Tibeto-Burman'. Tibeto-burman is a branch of Sino-Tibetan language family.

In Alexander Mackenzie's book it is written that "the inhabitants were of two very distinct classes, one of which, doubtless, originally came from China, but was now of the Hindoo persuasion; the other, a people call KooKies or Coocis". (*The North East Frontier of India*, A. Mackenzie, Reprint 1979/p. 275).

He further says that, "there would seem to be good reason for believing that the Kachari (Bada) race is a much more widely distributed one than it was at one time supposed to be. They are undoubtedly found well outside the limits modern (political) Assam, i.e. in North East Bengal Koch-Bihar, and also in Hill Tippera where the language of the people gives decisive evidence that they are of the Bada stock".

Dr. S.K. Chatterjee in his book *'Origin and Development of Bengali Language'* mentioned the Tripuri language as Tripura or Mrung'. In Tripura language 'SOM' means Salt, and 'DRU' means Salty water derived on centrifugal or admixture. Thus the SOM+DRU became ocean in Aryan word as Somudru, taking loan from Tripura words. Similarly, the word 'BANGLA' is Tripura language which means 'Earthquake'. So the name Bangladesh is also taken as loan word from Tripura language. The word RAJA, meaning king in English, is also Tripura word as considered from the explanation, as in Tripura language RA means 'Matured', JA means 'Leader' and JAK means 'Hand' i.e. Matured Hand. It explains the man having matured hand, capable of leading the race and to be throned in the kingdom.

We have assumed during our research, genuinely people of every culture want to know who their ancestors were and how their culture was built. But some claim without a research they originated from Aryan for just prestigious identity. The dialect spoken by those Mongoloids in the North-East India belong to SINO-TIBETO linguistic family. It has two sub-families :

a) Tibeto-Borok and b) Mon-Khmer.

Tibeto-Borok: North-East India is dominated by the Tibeto-borok linguistic family. It has 3 (three) sub-family linguistically. They are:-

a) Tripura or Korokborok and Boro or Bodo, it became dominant language in Tripura, Kachar, Brahmaputra valley, Borok valley in plains and hills. The people now speaking this language are Tripuras, Bodos, Garos, Mechs, and Rabhas etc.

b) Naga

c) Kuki-chin

It is clear from the above mentioned that, whole of the people inhabiting in North-East India constitute from one stock.

The Tripura dialect of the *Korokborok* language has kin relation to Bodo language group. The languages belonging to this group originated from the Sino-Tibeto sub-family of Tibeto-Borok language. The process of how the Tripura dialect has come into being with its root in the Sino-Tibetan language group. The following list of a few Tripura words with the Bodo language equivalent show the close connection of the vocabulary of two languages:

Table 6: Comparison of Language

Korokborok	*Bodo*	*English*
Ha	Ha	Earth
Tok	Dau	Bird
Sal	San	Sun
Twima	Duima	River
Matai	Mudai	God
Bukur	Bigur	Skin
Twi	Dwi	Water
Phikung	Bikhung	Back

Dr. Subhas Chottopadhyay regarding the close affinity of the nine dialects of Korokborok language is worth mentioning. According to him, "The extent of dialectical difference among the different dialects of Korokborok is not as wide as is found in the case of Bengali, English or German. The phonemic structures of the dialects of Korokborok are almost identical. Their grammatical structures are also wonderfully similar to each other. And the differences in their vocabulary are very negligible".

In Tripura dialect there are some terms that have same words totally or slightly but whose meanings are poles apart. It is perhaps common to all languages of the world. One of the richest languages of the world is English. Still in English there are many same words having compound meanings. For instance, the term SET in English has hundreds of meanings when used as nouns, verbs, and so forth. In like manner, Korokborok have several slight as well as exactly the same term but having different meanings no matter the same may be in prefix or suffix of the word. As to other language, the speaker has to identify the meanings in the context of the sentence where it is used. Some of the similar spellings that have different meanings can be seen as below:

Same words but different meanings:

	Korokborok	*English terms*
1.	Ah	a fish
	Ah	*ah!*
2.	Bw	he/she
	Bw	that
3.	Chok	peak
	Chok	dig
4.	Da	a heavy chopper
	Da	put in

5. Emang	dream
Emang	hopeless
6. Hor	night
Hor	carrying in back
7. Jora	joint
Jora	point
8. Kosong	length
Kosong	simple minded
9. Kwrwng	to meet together
Kwrwng	learned
10. Nog	you
Nok	a house
11. Sa	to speak
Sa	pain
12. Sam	grass
Sam	near
13. Sohk	burn
Sohk	reached
14. Tok	a bird
Tok	hit
15. Tui	water
Twi	carry

Parts of the Body :

Korokborok	*English*
Apuk	breast
Apuktwi	breast-milk
Bakhan	flesh
Bekreng	bone
Bwmwtwm	Brain

Bokhorok	head
Bokhok	mouth
Bubuk	intestine
Bukung	nose
Bukur	skin
Buwa	teeth
Bakha	heart
Bakhakwswm	liver
Bakhakuphu	lungs
Basak	body
Bwkhwmw	hair
Khakalap	chess
Khang-aa	cheek
Khi	stool
Khichalam	buttock
Khilam	anus
Khoklai	chin
Khilambunthu	rectum
Khukchi	lip
Khunju	ear
Kilinee	elbow
Bwlwi	penis
Lwitoktwi	testis
Mahang	face
Mokol	eye
Murku	eyebrow
Mwktwi	tear
Ok	belly
Omathai	navel

Sipak/tukui	vagina
Swhtwi	urine
Swhtwikhok	Urinary bladder
Taluka	forehead
Totra	throat
Thwi	blood
Yak	hand
Yakung-yaksi	toe
Yakora	heel
Yakung	leg
Yashu	knee
Yapha	palm
Yapalai	foot
Yaphatwk	thigh
Yaksi	finger
Yaksima	thumb finger
Yaksiyo	fore finger
Yaksichar	middle finger
Yaitam-yaksi	ring finger
Yaksi Kotoi	little finger
Yasukur	nail
Bachang	Waist
Phamokor	arm pit
Basakhok	Womb
Kotok bwchwlwi	Adam's apple
Salai	Tongue
Apuk bokhok	Nipple
Yakjora	wrist
Bakhan Konjya	muscle

Singari	Whiskers
Bramchai	Moustache
Khopchai	Beard
Sidduk	Veins/artery

A few connected words:

English	*korokborok*
Day	Sal
Morning	Phurung
Noon	Diphwr
Afternoon	Sarik
Evening	Swinda
Night	Hor
Dark-night	Hor-andar/manak
Mid-night	Horchar
Dawn	Aichuk
Today	Tini
Tomorrow	Khanab
Yesterday	Mia
Day before yesterday	Sone
Month	Tal
Year	Bishi
Hour	Tam mani/jora
Moon	Tal
Full Moon	Talpuni
Bright fortnight	Talpirshasa
Dark fortnight	Talthwimwrwrw
Lunar eclipse	Talmonok
Solar eclipse	Salmonok
Star	Handuk-khiri

Sky	Nokha
Rainbow	Choklengtwi
World	Swngsar

Some conjunction, Adjectives, Adverbs etc:

Korokborok	*English*
Arw	And
Matwr	But
Rwmdi	If
Tamahalai/ Tamanihwnba	Because
Baiphu	When
Araijahalai	Unless
Tophabo	Though/Although
Gam	Good
Arw-gam	Better
Hamkuk	Best
Hamjya	Bad
Jottoni Hamya	Worse
Hamjya-thak	Worst
Kebel	Weak
Machang	Beautiful
Katal	New
Kacham	Old
Gorja	Big
Kabang	Large
Kosha/bangya	Few/Little
Kwlwi	Soft
Kwchwng	Bright
Kolok	Long

Bara	Short
Kiting	Round
Bathab	Thick
Base	Thin

Riddles:

Buma bururok Basa tororok	Khul-kokuo
Nok bising uo Rwng chuk-uo.	Uaeng
Rajani kiship nu ship maya.	Purjyaa
Cheroksa kaiha achai matruo lakhub humuo.	Yaswkur
Tui bising uo alchuwai uo.	Shakamuk
Chanai dalu bobar barjya.	Muikhunchuk
Birnai toksa butui tuijya.	Tokbak
Cheroksa kainwi lama seklai uo.	Yakhung
Nok bising aru nok.	Musari
Rajani swnduk no khula khulok mao phung maya.	Toktui

Atmosphere:

Korokborok	*English*
Nobar	Air
Srai-srai	Clear
Chwmwi	Cloud
Kachang/Hing	Cold
Kutung	Hot
Karan	Dry
Kisi	Wet
Tungluluk	Warm
Hor	Fire
Watwi	Rain
Watwi-nobar	Storm

Nokhapilik-o	Lightening
Thatha	Thunder
Bangla	Earthquake

Colours:

Korokborok	*English*
Color	Rwng
Kwswm	Black
Kuphu	White
Kachak	Red
Chakshro-shro	Pink
Kakharang	Green
Swmlulu	Dark brown
Somchwnochwno	Light black
Kwrwmo	Yellow
Thapla	Ash
Chak-trutrue	Vermillion
Kachak-Swmlulu	Brown
Nokha rwng	Blue

Some Reptiles name in Tripura Korok :

Korokborok	*English*
Malnai	Reptiles
Chibuk	Snake
Sindrai	Centipede
Kerang	Tortoise
Sakamu	Snail
Songko	Conch
Markhimai	Crocodile
Nok Totobe	Lizard

Tote	Frog
Kenjua	Earthworm

Name of animals in Tripura korok (language)

Korokborok	*English*
Muphur	Bear
Misik	buffalo
Swi	Dog
Swima	Bitch
Musuk	Cow
Manging-gong	Camel
Aming	Cat
Mosong/Mwswi	Deer (big and small)
Mayung	Elephant
Shial	Fox/ Jackal
Purun	Goat
Korai	Horse
Wak	Pig
Masa	Tiger
Singho	Lion
Makhra	Monkey
Sinjo	Mouse/Rat
Masandwi	Porcupine
Mera	Sheep
Mandal	Squirrel
Gwnda	Rhinoceros
Tok	Bird
Tokla	Chicken

Different shapes of land in Tripura language :

Korokborok	*English*
Haraijo	Universe
Ha	Land\Earth
Hachen	Sand
Hapong Kuchuk	High Mountain
Hathai	Hill
Loma	Valley
Harung	Plain land
Hakor	Cave
Harep	Table land
Twima	River
Twisa	Rivulet\Stream
Dungur	Waterfall

Pronouns of korokborok :

Singular		*Plural*	
Korokborok	English	Korokborok	English
Ang	I	Chwng	We
Ani	My	Chini	Our
Nwng	You	Nog	You
Nini	Your	Nogni	our
Bo	He	Bog	They
Bini	His	Bogni	Their
Bono	Him	Bogno	Them

Some Tense :

Present Tense

Korokborok	English
Ang mai cha w	I eat rice
Nwng mai cha w	you eat rice
Bw mai cha w	He eat rice

Plural form :

Chwng mai cha w	we eat rice
Nog mai cha w	you eat rice
Bog mai cha w	they eat rice
Past Tense	
Ang mai chajak	I ate rice
Nwng mai chajak	you ate rice
Bo mai chajak	He ate rice
Present continuous tense	
Ang mai chawi tong-w	I am eating rice
Chwng mai chawi tong-w	we are eating rice
Nwng mai chawi tong-w	you are eating rice
Bo mai chawi tong-w	He is eating rice
Borog mai chawi tong-w	they are eating rice

Korok Parsi :

The korok-parsi is an interesting dialect of Tripuras. It has four types viz. i) Ri-Parsi, ii) Sipi-Parsi, iii) Ua-Parsi and iv) Taota-Parsi.

Example.

What is your name? (Ri-Parsi=Ri-ni Ri-mung Ri-ta Ri-ma Ri-lai)

(Ua-Parsi=Ua-ni Ua-mung Ua-ta Ua-ma Ua-lai)

Year, Month, day and week of the korokborok :

In korokborok year is called 'Bisi' and the month is called 'Tal'. The day is called 'Sal' and week is called 'Bar' in korokborok. The moon is also called 'Tal' and the Sun as 'Sal' in korokborok. The Tripuras follow calendar of Twipra/Tripura Bisi (Tripura Era) based on the collected data from different sources and the distinguished persons in a seminar on Twipra Bisi was organized by the Tripura Tribal Socio-Cultural Development Organization on December 1, 1991 at Tripura Public Service Commission Hall, Agartala. A book namely "The Historical Background of Tring (Tripura Era) published by KOKBOROK TEI HUKUMU MISSION may be as follows.

In this calendar, Talhing is the first month i.e. the 22nd December and Talbang (November 22) is the end of the month, AD of every year and the normal year would consist of 365 days and for every leap year would be 366 days.

The following is the length of the different months of Twipra Bisi calendar:

Month (Tal) in Gregorian caendar	*No. of days*	*Beginning date of the month*
1. Talhing	30 days	December 22 (in common year)
2. Talrung	30 days	January 21
3. Talsrang	30 days	February 20
4. Tallang	30 days	March 22 (31 days in a leap year)
5. Taltung	31 days	April 21
6. Talkran	31 days	May 22
7. Talyung	31 days	June 22
8. Taltuk	31 days	July 23
9. Talbang	31 days	August 23
10. Talumai	30 days	September 23
11. Taluang	30 days	October 23
12. Talbung	30 days	November 22

Origination of the names of months:

1. **Talhing**: Talhing is the beginning month of the winter. Hing means cold, from which the name of the month was coined.
2. **Talrung**: Harung is the plain cultivable land. During this time people gather out in the field for cultivation of some vegetables for their families' need.
3. **Talsrang**: This month usually represents the season autumn which is a refreshing session after a long winter months.
4. **Tallang**: Tallang is a month of clearance when all the bushes, jungles and surroundings are cleared.
5. **Taltung**: Taltung is coined from the word kutung. It is a month of heat.
6. **Talkran**: Talkran is taken from karan which means dry. It is the month of dryness.
7. **Talyong:** Yong means insects. It is a breeding month for different insects.
8. **Taltuk**: Taltuk is taken from the word kutuk which means immense growth. During this time the vegetations grow immensely.
9. **Talbang**: Talbang means kabang which means plenty. This time fruits grow in plenty.
10. **Talumai**: Talumai is the temperate month
11. **Taluang**: Uang is an animal which sounds in large number during this month.
12. **Talbang**: Talbang is taken from the word Kalbang. Kalbang is a traditional slightly cylindrical shaped made of bamboo cane. This is used during the time of harvesting for collection of different raw materials.

Name of the Days (SAL) :

Koktisal	= Sunday
Tangsal	= Monday
Kraksal	= Tuesday
Srangsal	= Wednesday
Sangrongsal	= Thursday
Phasal	= Friday
Chasal	= Saturday

Name of the Seasons (mol in Korokborok) :

Marsing Mol	= Winter Season
Tungphlama Mol	= Summer Season
Uatwi Mol	= Rainy Season
Sajalang Mol	= Autumn Season

Numerical Counting Method of Tripuras :

In *korokborok,* there is some peculiar form of numerals counting. In all the modern languages the word 'one' is used to mean one single irrespective of the article denoted. Thus it is one man, one hill, one bamboo, one rupee, one bird, one book, etc. But in korokborok it is not so. The numerals are classificatory in different objects with different terms. They used the word 'mag-ha' to denote 'one animal or bird'. For instance wak mag-ha which means one pig, Tok mag-ha = one bird, Swi mag-ha = one dog, Musuk mag-ha = one cow etc. In case of human they used different words to denote numerals as 'khorokha' which means 'one' for man and Woman. On the other hand to denote the numerals for inanimate objects like stick, log, bamboo, tree, flower, eye, leg, etc they use different kinds of words which are very interesting. For instance one stick = latha Kong-ha, one bamboo = WA Kong-ha, one tree = bophang phang-ha, etc. For instance flower, eye, and leg etc. numerical figures are used after the respective objects denote like one eye = Mokol kol-ha, one flower = Khum bar-ha etc. It is to be noted that for man and woman counted as Khorok, stick and bamboo as Kong, flower as 'Bar' and seeds as 'Kol' etc. to make clarification.

Thus the numerals of the Korok Borok may be arranged as follows :

One	-	Kaiha, mungha, kongha, phangha, kolha, barha, etc.
Two	-	kainwi, mungnwi, kongnwi, phangnwi, kolnwi, barnwi, etc.
Three	-	kaitham, mungtham, kongtham, phangtham, koltham, Bartham, etc.
Four	-	kaibrwi, mungbrwi, kongbrwi, phangbrwi, kolbrwi, Barbrwi, etc.
Five	-	kaiba, mungba, kongba, phangba, kolba, barba, etc.
Six	-	kaidok, mungdok, kongdok, phangdok, koldok, bardok, etc.
Seven	-	kaisni, mungsni, kongsni, phangsni, kolsni, barsni, etc.
Eight	-	kaichar, mungchar, kongchar, phangchar, kolchar, barchar, etc.
Nine	-	kaichiku, mungchiku, kongchiku, phangchiku, kolchiku, Barchiku, etc.
Ten	-	kaichi, mungchi, kongchi, phangchi, kolchi, barchi, etc.

In the market the Tripuras counted the rupee as 'Rang'

1	rupee	khok-ha
2	rupees	khok-nwi
3	rupees	khok-tham
4	rupees	khok-brwi
5	rupees	khok-ba

6 rupees	khok-dok
7 rupees	khok-sni
8 rupees	khok-char
9 rupees	khok-chiku
10 rupees	khok-chi

Counting Method of Korokborok:

1	Sha	One
2	Nwi	Two
3	Tham	Three
4	Brwi	Four
5	Ba	Five
6	Dok	Six
7	Sni	Seven
8	Char	Eight
9	Chiku	Nine
10	Chi	Ten
11	Chiha	Eleven
12	Chinwi	Twelve
13	Chitham	Thirteen
14	Chibrwi	Fourteen
15	Chiba	Fifteen
16	Chidok	Sixteen
17	Chisni	Seventeen
18	Chichar	Eighteen
19	Chi-chiku	Nineteen
20	Nwichi	Twenty
21	Nwichiha	Twentyone
30	Thamchi	Thirty

40	Brwichi	Forty
50	Bachi	Fifty
60	Dokchi	Sixty
70	Snichi	Seventy
80	Charchi	Eighty
90	Chukuchi	Ninety
100	Rasa	Hundred
200	Nwirasa	Two hundred
1000	Sai	Thousand
1,00,000	Rasai	One lakh
1,000,000	Chirasa	One million
10,000,000	Rwjag	Crore
1,000,000,000	Rarwjag	Billion

In conclusion, the entire above cited written documentary proved that, there is a Tribe Tripura since time immemorial and they have a unique of their mother tongue as *Korokborok*. The Tripura Tribe possesses itself a rich oral literature, song, legends, proverbs, etc. Linguists will be able to discover the vast treasure of their dialect if they study it as one of the sources of the origin and development of the Tibeto-Borok Sub-family of languages.

2

Socio-Cultural Dynamics of Tripura Tribe

The rich Cultural diverse existence is a unique identity of a race or tribe in the society of the nation. Man is born and brought up in a cultural environment. Man is born into a society is the same as saying that every man is born into a culture. Edward B. Tylor, a famous English anthropologist, has defined culture as " that complex whole which includes knowledge, belief, art, morals, law, custom and any other capabilities habit's acquired by man as a member of society". Peter Worsley, "Transmission of culture, the process whereby men learn the rules and practices of social groups". The Tripuras has also it own cultural heritage. The Socio-culture of Tripuras is the product of several million centuries. This society has high degree of fashion in dressing, production of cotton, weaving, use of verities of ornaments, etc. with cultural industries since immemorial. It has own aboriginal beliefs and customs. But in the medieval period influenced in many ways like, Muslim invasion, renaissance in Europe, first and second world war and lost of division as state and race lacking behind in education, Science, Philosophy and Technology. For that we find this Tribe of people always under changes as their religions, Titles and customs.

Globalization awakes the nation to evaluate their development in social, cultural, education, etc. The Tripura Tribe have adjusted themselves with Hindu as well as Christian in customary practices which differ from their traditional customs, rituals and rules of the original abodes.

Family

"Family is a group of persons united by ties of marriage, blood or adoption constituting a single household interacting and intercommunicating with each other in their respective social roles of husband and wife, father and mother, son and daughter, brother and sister, creating a common culture" (Burgees and Lock). Family plays an important role in the society of TRIPURA tribe. Family members live together under the one roof, by sharing love, joy and sorrow in the human made society of the world. In the world family is a place which is greater than all those man made religious holy places. Family is a place where we are born and brought up and also kept maintained as it is till the end of our life. After all family provides a learning environment for children, care and protects from which they received the belief, values of necessary and cultural behaviours for their own and their society's survivals. So, whom ever born in this world he/she has to enter in the boundary of family, otherwise it will be like a cup of tea without milk and sugar. Usually the structure and form of a family varies from one society to another. And family member's usually lived together but prior of education and other matters, children of some family's may settle periodically away.

The Tripura Community follows the patriarchal form of family structure. The father is the head and possesses all the authority of the family. The composition of the

Tripura family is nuclear type. The grown up children leave their parent's houses after attending adulthood and their marriages. After the marriage, the son starts a new family constructing a separate house generally adjacent to their parent's house. It is also found that even after marriage, the son along with daughter-in-laws jointly live in the parent's house for the required period. The eldest son does not separate himself from the parent's establishment. On the death of the father, the eldest son becomes the head of the family. The mother of the family also performs her duties of the guardian, till the children grow up on the event of the expiry of her husband.

In the Tripura Community, a family consists of the father, mother and the unmarried children. It is however observed that, in addition to the above members the old-aged parents, close relatives such as nephew, niece also live with the family. Though the father is the head of the family and possesses all the authorities in the family, he too exercises power in consultation with his wife. This authority does not wax or wave during his old age. All the members of the family are bound to follow his direction and must seek advice from him for all sorts of activities concerned with the family. Being the head of the family the father performs all the socio-religious rituals of the family. He is responsible to the overall welfare of the whole family members including their fooding, clothing and education of the children. All earnings by the individual members of the family go to the account of the father. However, the wife and the grown up children in a family are allowed to keep their own individual share of their earning to meet the requirements according to their own. The wife i.e. the housewife helps her husband in the discharge of his duties, especially in the household affairs such as cooking of food, rearing of household animals, fetching of drinking water and firewood, collection of consumable vegetable from the jungle etc. Besides, the housewife is also responsible for weaving cloths to meet the requirement of the family members and also to offer gifts to the kith and kin during the occasion of festivals and other social occasions.

The father being the head of a family is responsible for all sorts of activities. The grown up sons assist their father in the Huk cultivation, construction of dwelling house and other family activities. Likewise, the grown up daughters also extend help to their mother in cooking of foods, fetching of drinking water, firewood etc.

On the event of death of the head of the family the responsibility of the head of the family is vested to the widow of the deceased husband in case no adult children are available at the time of expiry of the father. The widow, while shouldering responsibility of the family always consults her close relatives in maintenance of the family. But as soon as a widow remarriage with another person the overall responsibility is automatically vested to her new husband. In a family the orphan family members are looked after by the widow and take the burden of overall maintenance of the orphans without any hesitation.

As is mentioned before there are distinctive nature of duties of the father and rest of the members of the family, thereby there is a division of labour existing in the Tripura Society as is prevalent in all the other tribal and non-tribal societies. In a Huk cultivator family all the adult members of the family actively participate in all the activities of the huk cultivation barring the minor children. The minor children in a family remain in the house when the adult members are away in the huk field. The minor children take responsibility and care of the kids and babies besides rearing of household animals.

The responsibility of maintenance of the family in the Tripura Society is vested to the head of the family i.e., the father. After the death of the father, the grown up or major sons, take over the responsibilities to maintain the whole family including his widowed mother. If the son has not yet grown up, the 'Sandai', Close relatives on the paternal side, takes over the responsibility of their family till the children attains adulthood.

Nature of Family

The Tripuras have followed both joint and nuclear family system. Before globalization joint family was more in vogue than the nuclear family. All though both types of family are still practiced, nuclear family system is dominant in the present modern society. Birth control, family control, flexible demands and fascinated human mind lead occupied on nuclear system of family. In Tripuras, the authority of the family is entirely vested to the eldest male in the family. The eldest male can be a great-grand father, grand father, father, as well as an eldest son. He controls whole family members in all matters whether great and small. In other words, his say on any matters is the supreme and final, normally without any question.

The nuclear family increase in the globalized society; it is due to the result of split of the joint family. In the Tripuras, the nuclear family is established normally on the basis of mutual agreement in the family. Some family on certain cases, a couple after having one or two children sought for a separate family. If the proposal is accepted, then that particular couple with their children establish a new house and maintain a nuclear family. They are offered some properties from the family for their basic and urgent needs. Subsequently, this family become an independent family in their own affairs. In respect of love and relationship of families is same to other tribes.

Role of the Eldest Male in the Family

As stated earlier the eldest male member in the family can be the great-grand father, grand father, father or the eldest son. Legally and practically, the father is the head of the family whether it is joint or nuclear family system.

In Tripura language father is called 'BAGWI'. In the family, the duty of Father is to look after economic, education, health and spiritual affairs. In other words, father is the responsibility overall welfare of the family. He administers and maintained all the properties of the household. His decision is always supreme and final.

No matter how much weak educationally, physically and intellectually, he is still the father of the family whose voice is supreme. He punishes and rebukes any member of the family going against the norms and discipline of the family. In the absence of the head, the second eldest male of the family have to look after the family. All the hard works such as construction of house, ploughing the paddy field, cutting the forest for huk etc., are done by the male members of the family. Father is main key for smooth functioning of the family. The male members co-operate internally as well as externally in the society.

Role of the Mother in the Family

Mother also plays an important role in the family of Tripuras. The contribution made by mother in the family is no less in anyway. She is an assistant to the father (husband). Mother look after household works at home and beyond that she care the children in their upbringing. Mother have to play dual role. She is a mother as well as teacher. The mother trains her daughters in all womanly arts and crafts like cooking, weaving, knitting etc. Mother has to work husking paddy, collecting firewood, fetching water, preparing rice beer, cooking, washing and many other domestic works. Besides that she has to work in huk for planting, sowing, weeding, harvesting, reaping, etc. The daughters help their mother in domestic works, go to school and also care after younger brothers and sisters.

In case father died, mothers become responsible to look after family as well as children until they become mature enough to take in-charge.

Types of House

The traditional houses of Tripura Tribe are *Gaireng, Char-nok, Bera-nok* and *Gudam nok,* with the influence of industries at present people constructed building houses. The Gaireng constructed in the huk for the period of few season. The Char-nok is constructed at hillock as well as plan land. Both the houses are constructed by bamboo, wood and son-grass is used as roof. This type of house is build about seven to eight feet high. The lower part of the house is kept with free spaces, where domestic animals are kept. One-fourth or one-third of a house kept open and almost free. The remaining part of the house is walled up, the walls being made woven by bamboo spilt. In this huts we find one door and there is no windows. Bera-nok is constructed in plain land as well as in hillock for permanent. It is also constructed by wood, bamboo and for the roof it is used son-grass as well as tin. This type of house also have no windows, but it has two or three doors. The *Gudam-nok* (mud-walled house) is constructed by mud wall and wood, bamboo, son-grass, tin is used to construct roof. It has door as well as windows. It usually last for 10 to 20 year approximately depending upon its use.

Physical Features

Ethnologically the Tripuras belong to Tibeto-Borok stock having marked Mongolian feature. Their physical characteristics are also akin to the other tribes of Tripura. They have medium stature, well built physique, broad head, small eye, flat nose depressed at the base and scanty hair. They have had flat face and thick lip. Their complexion varies from yellow-brown to light brown. The female is calmly and little shorter in stature. It may be noted here that all of them are not of same stature.

By character and nature, they are meek, simple minded and hospitable. They are honest, truthful in deeds and works. They are hard working as well as efficient cultivators. They are devoid of all violence towards their own people and their neighbours.

Food and Drinking Habits

The Tripuras' food items are a mixture of both vegetarian and non-vegetarian food articles. Like many other tribes of Tripura, their method of preparing food is very simple. Tripuras generally, grow crops at homestead, Huk-ow (huk), Pathur-ow (wet land) and wild harvest. For both non-vegetarian and vegetarian, the principal crop and staple food is RICE.

The food are prepared delicious by using spices with less oil, pasty and other popular items like Gudog, Chakhrwi, Mwituru, Mwkhwrwi etc. and verities of paddy.

The myriad forest produces used as food by different tribal communities of Tripura are diverse in nature and form the part and parcel of their unique dietary pattern and choice. The major kinds of vegetable used in preparing food items are various types of roots, leaves, flowers, fruits and stems. Tasty vegetables collected from nearby forest edible plants and aromatic plants are Mwi-ua (bamboo shoots), Tharai (tara), Orai (Betel leave like curry patta), Gandri, Laiphang, Mwicheng, Gong^a bochok, Thakun, phaunma, Thabalai kiting, mwikhumchok, kenchiri, Sakumu-bakalab, usundwi, logbanda, sipling, etc. During the monsoon, bamboo-shoot is widely used as an alternative food material.

All kinds of Ah (fish), Ah karan (dry fish), Mikhan (meat), and milk and poultry products are food taken by them.

Various kinds of wild edible fruits thaicherem, Amila, Thaitoi, Thailob, Kok, Dedowai, Thaimachang, Kwswmai, Boroi bolong, jam, Thaichok bolong, etc.

Domestic edible fruits are Thaipong, Thaichok, Lechu, Boroi, Goyang, Jam, kuwai, Jambora, Narke, Thailik,

Mongphol, Thaichumu, Daramai, Khira, Sosha, etc.

The chief spices used by the Tripuras are Mwsw (chilli), Silik (Turmeric), Khumsaini (Huk Dania), Haicheng (Ginger), Bakhwr (Dania), Piyai (Onion), Thok(oil), Tejlai(cardamom) and many other fragrant spices are found in their food.

Chakhrwi (A type of vegetable dish cooked with locally prepared soda)

Bamboo shoot is one of the favourite food items of Tripuras. Bamboo shoot curry is prepared in both bamboo pipe and cooking pot. They also prepare a special type of curry with alkaline substance out of the ashes of burnt bamboo and mustard plant called Chakhrwi.

Mwkhwrwi (A type of sour tasting vegetable dish)

Sour curry is called 'Mwkhwrwi' in Tripura dialect. It is prepared by them with a kind of sour vegetable fruit or leaf which they produce profusely in the huk.

Gudog (An indigeneous non-veg mixed dish)

Another famous food item prepared by Tripuras is known as Gudog. Gudog curry is prepared in the green bamboo pipe. The process of preparing the item is very interesting one. The Gudog curry can be prepared with meat, fish and different kinds of vegetables. To prepare it, no spices or oil is necessary. Only salt, chilli and turmeric are necessary to prepare it. Sometimes they use green coriander in it to add flavour to it. Nowadays, Gudog became famous food item among the other group of people of Tripura also.

They also procure and preserve the fat of boar used for frying vegetable and cakes. The fat is also used as medicine as a curative measure for chronic pain in any part of the body.

Awan (cake)

There is no elaborate process of preparing cakes among Tripuras. Cakes are baked from 'Gabi' (a kind of rice powder). The cake is prepared both from normal rice and fragrant rice. The awan are:

1. Awan pongjak (A type of steamed cake)

Awan Mayrong (rice) wet by soaking in water is put into an earthen pot with perforated bottom. It is now placed on another earthen pot containing water. A lid is placed on the upper pot. Sometimes mud lining is applied where the two pots join to prevent the escape of vapour from the pot below. Now it is heated over an oven. The rice in the upper pot is cooked with the vapour rising from the pot below. The cake baked in this way is known as Awan pongjak.

2. Awan perengjak (A type of boiled cake prepared out of whole rice or rice flour)

Awan Mairong is washed and soaked in water and then stuffed into a Wasung (bamboo pipe) and baked on burning charcoal until ready for serving.

3. Awan bathai (A type of boiled cake specially prepared in leaves)

It is prepared and taken during winter and different occasion. The Gabi or Awan-Mairong is wrapped in laidob balai, gwrjwng balai and Thailik balai (kinds of leaf used specially for this purpose) and left on burning charcoal for baking. In winter morning it is quite delicacy.

Traditional drinks made of rice are chuwak, chuwakma bwtwi, kata and baramji (tpes of local made wine) which are used for both social and religious purposes. They have customary practice to offer wine in the worship and entertaining guests of respectable position. This wine is prepared at home by Tripura womenfolk. They never buy or take wine from the market.

Wine is use in festivals and rituals; this tradition is considered harmful and rejected in modern day because it has an impact on economy and work. Beyond that it is water which every body need for life survival. And they also like to take tea and coffee.

Smoking is also common to Tripuras, man and woman. For smoking they use 'Daba' (hubble-bubble). Daba is prepared by bamboo pipe. They also smoke bidi.

Tripuras also have the habit of chewing betel leaf and areca nut, they buy it from market.

Dresses and Ornament

Traditionally Tripura tribe wears very simple dress which is similar to that of their tribal counterparts living in the state Tripura. The difference in sight is in terms of colouring and designing. Normally traditional dresses of womenfolk consist of two pieces of unstitched cloth. These two pieces of cloth make complete garments. The complete garments are divided into upper and lower dress. The upper is called 'RISA' and the lower is 'RINAI'. Rinai is used to the lower part of body as petty cot with black and red combination and some with different arts, handicrafts designs. Risha which is used to cover her breasts with splendid artistic designs. Traditionally Risha and Rinai is woven with high skilled by woman. Mother presented Rinai and Risa to her daughter-in-law during marital ceremony to show love and affection, also as a token of acceptance as bride. The male wear 'Tenja' and 'Rematwi' (dhuty) lower part of their body and Kanchilik/ Kobai (as shirt) to cover Upper part of their body. Meyasow is like a sleepless shirt worn by man. And in the head they tied with Risa which is known as 'Khorok sormani Risa'. Khwrwm and Yakalap is made of wood, which is used at the foot. Besides that, they wear Repa during winter to get relief from cool.

They prefer red, yellow and black colour to any other colours. Therefore these three-colour combinations are found predominant in their Rinai and Risa. The Rinai and Risa are woven out of their home spun thread in their loin looms. Formally every Tripura household had been in possession of one or two spinning wheels. Both male and female attires are woven in their loin-loom. They also make shirt from the cloth they weave for both male and female to use in the huk. The female folk generally use rinai and risa. Both of this does not make complete garment--therefore the female uses mill-made blouse mostly black and red in colour.

Apart from the above mentioned dresses, Tripuras have more dresses to use at different times and occasions. They are as follows :

Rituikluk : It is a piece of cloth like a towel used by males at the time of taking bath.

Khoroksa : It is a head dress or turban which is commonly used by all Tribal and by Indians. In Tripuras it is used by both male and female at different occasions such as huk work, dancing, worshiping and wedding ceremony. It is made either at home or cloth mill.

Kanchilik : It is a shirt made of mill cloth. They buy it from market. Kanchilik is not different from the common shirt used by all modern people.

Repa : It is a kind of woollen cloth worn during winter. It is woven at home and also bought from market.

Birki : It is a bed sheet made of homespun yarn. It is also used as wrapper by both the sexes in the winter.

Jewellery

The Tripura woman is very fond of jewellery. She likes very much to adorn herself with a variety of jewellery mostly made of silver and beads bought from smith. She wears a variety of bangles, armlets, necklaces, ear rings, nose rings and pendant etc. The male do not wear ornaments. They only wear finger ring. All ornaments worn by Tripuras are made of splendid design.

The ornament worn by Tripura women are--Narchaing, Toya, Jajana, Nabak, Wakhum (in ears), Naphu, Bali (in nose), Bengi (in legs), Mathia, Bangiri brap, Bangiri (in hands), Rangbatang, Tusa, Sashiri (in neck), Chem (waist), Sang^aa , Surang, Khajur maduri (in hair). Globalization and industrialization have made life with full of fashion which influenced among Tripura tribe also. The man, in present day wears long pant and shirt with varying designs, even cot and tie in the important occasions. Women are more influenced by fascinated society of world.

Some details of the ornaments worn by Tripuras are as follows :

Wakhum : It is a flower like ornament with a barrel-shaped bar at the backward which is stuck to the perforation of the lobe of the ear. It is made of silver.

Toya : It is alike oleander-flower bud-shaped. It is worn on the upper ear with the projection upward. To wear Toya a perforation is made in the middle of the upper part of the ear. It is also made of silver.

Naphu : The generic name for the nose ornament. It is a nostril stick with a ball and flower made at the top. It is worn on the right side of the nose base.

Bali : It is a nose pendent worn in the middle part of the nostril. Bali is generally made of silver.

Mathia : It is a generic name for a bangle. Tripura womenfolk wear a variety of bangles massive and thin on the wrist. They are known as Bangiri brap, Bangiri etc.

Neck-ornaments : Tripura woman wears a variety of necklace long and short in sizes. The necklaces are mostly made of silver. Ornaments are as :

Rangbatang/Rangbak : Rang means coin and batang means wreath. It is a threaded silver coin. It is a very favourite and prestigious necklace of Tripura women.

Khumtang : This necklace is made ot different kind flowers. It is used during honour programme of Ruwaja, pomang, Naran, etc. It also symbolises the very liking for flowers.

Yaksitam : It is a finger-ring. The ring is simple in design and made of silver and gold.

Bengki : It is worn in the anklet. These are made of massive silver with narrow neck being a conical shape of both the ends. This ornament is well designed.

Surang : It is a hairpin generally used by the spinster made of animal horn or bone. The top end of it is much larger than that of the opposite end and which is pointed. The surang is generally made for gift to the lady love by the lover.

Sang^a : It is a hair clip commonly used by the Tripura women folk to keep tightened the khajur. It is a two-pronged clip made of silver or aluminium with the annular shape on the top end wherein are stuck metallic rings or the copper piece or the round piece of aluminium. It is to be noted that all the ornaments are made and sold by goldsmith.

Musical Instruments

Tripuras are endowed with innate love for music and dance. They have several kinds of musical instruments of their own. These musical instruments are mostly made and manufactured by themselves. Musical instruments are important for vocal as well as dance recital. Dance and song can not be performed without accompaniment of musical instruments. These people are very expert to play melodious music without any training for notation on the instruments. It is surprising to note that they can play any kind of instrument to the tune of any vocal music.

The musical instruments prepared and used by Tripuras are :

Sumwl (flute) : Sumwl literally means flute. It is very popular musical instrument of Tripuras. Traditionally Tripura tribe youth have innate love to play note of romantic love-song by flute. The very nocturnal solitude of Tripura villages is gently broken by the echo of lifting melodies of sumwl. Though the sumwl is played to the accompaniment of love-song, it is also played on to the accompaniment of different dance recitals like goria, huk, and other kind of dances.

Chongpreng (Indigeneous guitar) : It is a stringed musical instrument made of wood. Chongpreng is manufactured by the artiste themselves. It is purely indigenous musical instruments of Tripuras. It is also played to accompaniment of vocal recital or creating orchestral symphony and other recitals. In the modern age, people preferred guitar manufactured by factories instead of chongpreng.

Duluk and Madol (Drum) : It is literally known as Drum. It is very popular among the tribes. The Duluk and Madol are played on the occasions of music and dance recital. This is also beaten on funeral and other ceremonial occasions. The Duluk is generally small in size and the Madol can be big and small in sizes. It is made of wood of which both ends are covered with cowhide.

Dangdu (Jaw harp) : It is a kind of mouth organ made of iron rod, the frame having an annular base which does not complete the circle. The ends of the incomplete ring project into two prongs. A thin tongue is fixed in between the two prongs which are kept free at the terminal end. This Dangdu in English is called jaw's harp, though there is no resemblance to the harp at all. To play Dangdu it is needed to set in between the upper and lower tips of the player. The player is to hold the base of it in one hand and is to beat by the index finger of other hand on the hook-shaped end of it. While beating finger on the hook the player has to make sound by oral breathing thereby resonating gentle sound.

Apart from above mentioned musical instruments Tripuras have also made musical instruments like *Mechong, tok-tui-khereng,* etc. These instruments are traditionally used and of special significance and associated with Tripura custom and culture in a unique sense.

Festival and Folk Dance

The traditional festivals and cultural functions performed by Tripura Tribe are considered to be of high standard. It is celebrated with folk songs, dances, musics and folk games of specialities. The important national festivals of Tripura Tribe are *Hari buisu, Buisu, Bisi katal, Mainungma,* etc. which is celebrated by mass people in the society.

Bwisu (a name of Festival)

Buisu is one of the most important festivals of Tripuras. It is celebrated by all the Tripuras at the end of the yearly harvest in the month of mid-April, when all the people are free from their field works having gathered all the crops. The time usually falls on the autumn season with all the birds singing in the air, especially the koel. The sound of koel is very much related to the Buisu festival. The busy Tripuras awakes at the hear of koel and come to know that Buisu is at hand. So are prepared for it at their best possible way. Buisu Festival last normally for two days. The first day which is the Buisu eve is known as Hari buisu. The last day is the main day of Buisu.

On Hari Buisu, many important occasions take place. This day is the important day for the youths. They perform some rites. On this day the young females are given the honour by putting Risha. They are then recognized as mature enough to get married. At present, with the development in every field taking place, age limits are given and looked into as for the case of maturity and marriage of girls and boys. The households are purified and all the domestic animals are tied around with garlands as a measure of showing respect and honour for their hard work throughout the whole year and producing good crops. It is also a time seeking blessing for the coming year. Youths makes some cakes from sticky rice and other good quality rice in varieties as for enjoyment and to be taken by all the members of the house and any visitors. The elders are also given bath or feet washed by the younger generation and blessings are sought from them. They are then bowed with respect with a bottle of wine as gift.

On the **main Buisu** day, the first duty of every individual is to purify themselves by taking a dip in the water. A type of secret competition is there among them as to who can refresh first by taking a dip at hear of the first sound of the koel. A lot of drinking and eating best food takes place that day. On this day in every home good food and other eatables, cakes especially will be found. The most common food item is chicken cooked with rice pestle called Gabi. It is also a time of social gathering and family meet together as this day is the last day of the year and being well lived. It last till the final and the ending day of the buisu. Wine drinking is very common among Tripuras. So during this day, it is allowed and offered every where.

Goria Dance

This is a unique and main dance of the Tripuras. This is performed by a group of youths mainly male. Some of the youths take part in this dance. With much effort this dance is practiced for about a month or weeks, for best performance in the buisu festival. It is a dance for pleasing the Goria god. Some say that Goria is a god of fun. So in this dance all sort of fun and dirty jokes are played as a custom. For some groups, it takes three days, where they move out on Hari Buisu and come home on next day of Buisu after going around from house to house the main Goria Kol(where Goria is believed to be present) in every possible village. For some it takes on week.

Since 2002 Buisu festival is celebrated together jointly at state level, which organised by the Tripura Chubalai Buthu, Goria dance is performed by various sub clans of Tripuras and sub-divisions and measures for improvement are found out. Other traditional games and sports are also performed as a part of traditional practice. Views are also always kept for improvement and broadcast it up to the international level of Tripura community. Mainungma is another important festival which is celebrated in the month of October.

The folk dance of Tripuras are *Goria, Huk Tangmani,* etc. which are lively and attractive. These dances are performed during the festival of Buisu.

Folk Sports

Tripura Tribe have their own traditional games and sports. The term sports in Tripura language is known as 'Thungma'. The sports entertain children and youth in every time. Nowadays though the Tripura children have adopted the other castes' games and sports, still it is played at least once in a blue moon. Some traditional games and sports of Tripura community are discuss below:

a) cherok mai-mwi songlaimani (Cooking game)

The Tripuras children are fond of cooking game the first stage of game of all society children plays. It is played by collecting different leaves, roots, mud, sand, water etc. they pretend to prepare different curry and rice with water. Bamboo slits, little pieces of tree roots etc. they use as fire wood. When the pretended preparation is over, they pretend to serve it among others or to eat it by themselves.

b) Ua suglaimani (push wrestling)

This is a push wrestling played by two individuals or groups. A bamboo pole is taken to play this game. The players stand at a specific distance from each other. A mark is put in the middle. The two ends of the bamboo pole are then placed under their right armpit and each grasps it firmly by both hands. Now-both the players try to cross over the marking between them by pushing back each other.

c) Achukwi phran-Swlaimani (A type of wrestling by sitting)

It is a type of wrestling played by two young men to test their strength. The two young men sit on the ground facing each other and spread their legs. Then they began to pull each other. He who is able to pull his side wins the game.

d) Dul-laimani (Wrestling)

Dul-laimani literally means wrestling. This is a kind of free hand wrestling. The objects of this wrestling is to subdue or turndown the opponent by grasping each others chest with their hands and legs. It is an individual game played by two individual against each others.

e) Huijaklaimani (Hide and seek)

This is a collective game played by children. The children hide in different places according to their scope and one among the players remains as seeker, who tries to find out the hider one. Among the hiders the leader will give a signal after they manage to hide themselves. Then the seeker starts searching to find out the hiders. The hider who is traced out first by the seeker will be in turn as next seeker. As a result, the game is started afresh by rotation and everyone is likely to become a seeker.

f) Buduk swtwnlaimani (Tug of war with rope)

This game is habituated to be played by both the children and youths. Buduk swtwnlaimani literally means 'Tug of war'. It is played with pleasure for trial of strength. In an open field or in the courtyard they lay this game. The boys divide themselves into two groups. A long rope is taken and each party stands in a line one after another by holding the rope firmly at their respective side. The group which can pull their opponent towards them across a particular mark lying between the parties wins the game.

g) Tokla Tanlaimani (An indigineous game imitating cocks-cockfight)

This is an individual game; they pretended to fight each other as cocks. They make a boundary in the courtyard or in the plain land and all participants assemble in that arena. In this game player hold his ankles by bending one leg at the knee and holds an ear by another hand. Then they dash one another by jumping on a single leg. At the time of dashing, if any body's leg or ear slips from the grip or if he crosses the boundary he is declared loser.

h) Sukui thwngmani (A game using the seeds of a wild creeper)

This game used to be played with the seeds of Sukui (a wild creeper bean). The seeds are flat and of round shaped. The colour of the seed is brown with a patch of black. To play this game, a clean plane land is needed. A line parallel with the side line of the field is drawn on another side of the field. Within this line the Sukui are set in vertical position maintaining distance of 2 inches between them. Another parallel line is drawn at a distance of six to seven cubits from the *previously drawn line. This type of game has five stages as danha, dannwi.*

The number of players of this game is not fixed. This game can be played by two groups or more. The numbers of players depend upon the numbers of Sukui. The players of both sides are to strike the beans kept erect on the line. The player is to grip the Sukui with his thump and forefinger. To strike them by throwing sukui with right hand through the gap created by holding the toe of the lifted right leg with the left hand bending down his body. If the game takes place between two individuals, if a player fails to strike the beans kept on the line, then his opponent's turn comes. But, if it is played group- wise' then if a player fail to strike the bean another players of the same group attempt serially to strike the bean. This game is played in different occasion till today.

Marriage System of Tripuras

The term Marriage in korokborok is 'KAIJAKMA'. Marriage is socially approved for family and sharing anything between a man and a woman. In other words marriage can be defined as a socially approved sexual and economic union relation between opposite sexes. It is universally practiced in every section of societies, but system of practices is different from one society to another. Thus, every section of community of this world has its own set norms and practices of do's and don'ts. Marriage plays an important role of human life with its difference in characteristics in the society of the world. Edward Westermarck in his "History of Human Marriage" defined marriage as "the more or less durable connection between male and female lasting beyond the mere act of propagation till after the birth of offspring". Alfred McClung lee defined marriage as, "Marriage is the public joining together, under socially specified regulations of a man and woman as husband and wife".

In Tripura community the rule of monogamy is followed in their society. Marriage between individuals of the same clan is possible. It is believed that, through such marriages the closeness within the same clan increases with chances of less misunderstanding amongst each other. In the Tripura community clan endogamous is preferably practiced. Among the Tripuras, marriage within the same clan is preferred, but in course of advancement of the society inter-tribal community marriage is also acceptable. Marriage outside the tribal community is also in existence in the Tripura Community especially among the enlightened youths those who are associated with the white-collar profession.

In the whole social custom of the Tripura community there are customary rules for excommunication from the society because of inter-tribal community marriage. But this practice of inter-tribal community marriage is almost in existence in the present Tripura society. In the Tripura society, the marriage or matrimonial alliance with other religion is allowed as in the present day context. However, it is observed that in such marriages the bride is always converted or has to comment to the religion of the bride groom.

According to the Tripura customary laws the engagement system is also there in existence. This engagement system generally takes place through negotiation with the appointed intermediaries for such negotiation in between the guardians of the bride and the bridegroom.

Once the engagement ceremony is solemnized, the parents of both the bride and bridegroom are under compulsion to go ahead for the marriage of their son or daughter. On the event of departure or non fulfillment of engagement, the defaulting party is liable to pay fine and also to compensate the expenditure so incurred by the other party as decided by the Village Council under the headship of the 'Ruwaja' of the concerned village.

Traditionally, there are six distinctive ways of acquiring mates in the Tripura Community.

1. Marriage by negotiation,
2. Marriage by elopement,
3. Marriage by close interaction between an adult boy and a girl or love marriage.
4. Marriage by Service and
5. Widow/Widower marriage.
6. Forced Marriage

Polygamy and polyandry are not practiced in the Tripura society. Bigamy is also strictly prohibited in the society. Marriages by the way of elopement are not accepted in the society unless and until it is followed by performance of the formal marriage ceremony confronting the social customs.

In the Tripura society the children of the agamas union is also acceptable, but agamas union is of a rare phenomenon in the society.

Monogamy (single marriage) as social norms was and is in practice since time immemorial. This monogamous practice does not necessarily relate to the sex ratio or economic status of the Tripura community.

As have been mentioned earlier polygamy (a man having more than one wife) is not allowed in the Tripura community. If any person of the Tripura society practices polygamy, he is liable to be punished by imposing fine as prescribed by the village Council under the headship of the village 'Ruwaja/Choudhury'.

Marriage within the close relatives is not permissible, such as between cross cousin and parallel cousin, marriage and between uncle and niece etc.. In fact marriage among close relatives up to the second generation is prohibited. The same restriction is imposed in case of marriages between the aunt and nephew. If it has taken place, then they are liable to be punished by imposing fine as prescribed by the village council under the headship of the village 'Ruwaja'.

The Tripura society have strong social bond. All the members of the society are under compulsion to adhere to the social customs and rituals but in the modern age and by the influence of globalization, the adult grown up youth can also go ahead of marriage among themselves even without the concurrence and prior consultation with concerning parents or legal guardian.

Since the social bondage is diminishing the imposition of fine and punishment is not associated in the marriages which takes place without the prior consent or concurrence of the guardian.

Marriage between fosterage group of people like father and step daughter or mother and step son or adopted son or daughter and foster brother or sister is totally prohibited among the Tripuras.

The matrimonial relationship in the lineage of the father or of the mother up to second generation is totally prohibited in the Tripura community.

In Tripura community there is no specific marriageable age bar as prescribed, the only thing is that the couple must be efficient and skilful. Traditionally, as long as the young boys is not physically able for huk cultivation and young girls were not fully equipped without the Risa ceremonial done to the particular girl, beyond that should have the cooking ability and weaving of cloth, without this basic things there is no question of marriage to any girls in Tripura society.

However, by the conforming of the modern society, the bride groom should attain at least 21 years of age and the bride must attain 18 year of age at the time of marriage. Among the Tripura youths, especially the educated ones, the age of marriage is ever rising and is always conforming to the social establishment. Child marriage is totally prohibited.

Once the marriage ceremony takes place between a bride and bridegroom conforming to the social customs, it is recognized by the society. The husband and the wife are conferred with the legal status for all purposes in the Society.

Marriage which takes place without the social customs and recognition, have no right to claim or enjoy social status until such illegal marriage is accepted by the society through the way of performance of social marriage and payment of fine in terms of punishment as inflicted by the Village Council.

In the traditional marriage of Tripuras there are some norms which are practiced among the youth. Tripura clan has been divided into five Desw. They are :

1) Baklap Desw. 2) Bokorong Desw.

3) Ramwk Desw, 4) Kuchuk Desw and

5) Gul Desw.

The Desw has a sole role in the marriage ceremony, when there is inter-marriage held between two Desw then the particular bride's Desw youth may charge groom Desw with fines called hachi as per their norms. The different hachi (fined goods and services) demanded by different Desw are –

a) **Baklap Desw** : Kuwai bathai (Betel-nut) 12x20x12nos, 12 bakhlak, 12 berchek and 12 biphring,

b) **Bokorong Desw** : Surang 9 sin (1sin=1 finger in breadth) one pair and 5 sin one pair,

c) **Ramwk Desw** : Mala (Garland) 7 mod (1mod= 1 handfold in length)

d) **Kuchuk Desw**: Surang 7 sin 1 pair and 5 sin 1 no.

e) **Gul Desw** : Betara (comb) 5 piece.

If the above mentioned hachi are not given even after quite a number of appointed days, the culprit are liable to be put to shame and clothes may be stripped off.

Daphal/Bokshis (a kind of dowry)

Mother and father of bride also demand as Daphal, an amount of money or things to the groom parents. And of course bottles of wine or pairs of coconut for the Elders of bride, both the married and unmarried as well as male and female. In modern day this practices was seen very rare.

Details about Daphal or Bokshis :

Father	Mother
Rs. 5/-	Rs. 5/-
Rematwi' (dhuty) 1nos.	Rinai 1nos.
Kanchilik/ Kobai 1nos.	Risa 1nos.
Chuwak 1bottle.	Chuwak 1 bottle

Chuwak-kaw (Engagement ceremony)

In the Tripura community, if the parents of the bride and bride groom or proposed bride and bride groom put up proposal for any marriages to their counter part, it shall be through a ceremony known as 'Chuwak-kaw'.

a) According to existing Customary Rules Chuwak-kaw ceremony is generally performed in the evening.

b) On the appointed date the guardian of the proposed bridegroom along with a few of his friends shall visit the house of the parents of the bride taking with him bottles of country liquor including some sweets, etc. and ceremonially put forward the proposal for the marriage.

c) If the guardian of the bride agrees to such proposal, the date of the marriage ceremony shall be finalized on that occasion itself.

d) Alternatively the guardians of the bride may not communicate their decision on the date but it may be communicated subsequently.

e) In case the guardians of the bride keep reserved the declaration of the date of marriage, in such situation the guardian of the bride groom shall depute messenger for confirmation of the proposal.

Khobor (information)

In Tripura society there is also practice as information like Khobor Gurasa and Khobor Gorja after marriage. In Khobor Gurasa the parents of the groom came to meet bride parents. There is a dialect, *"Nini basanw tokleng tilangya, masa bw uarjya Ani basa bai se jora mapa ongw. Nok boma bopha ong-wi tongmaniba ma saphai mani-se"*. In this time groom parents carried two bottles of wine with them one for bride parent and another for Ruwaja on that particular village. In this meeting bride parents demands above mentioned things as a whole to bring at the time of *Khobor Gorja*. *Khobor Gorja*- this time groom has to visit to bride parents with groups of elder and youth both male and female. They carry along with them all the things which demand has been made during Khobor gurasa. And they also carry Chuwak potta, Toksa, Awan, etc. with them.

Some different types of marriages have been briefly discuss below :

Bwrwi nai-wi kaijakmani/ Boma-Bopha Kaimani (Arranged marriage)

This is a kind of negotiated marriage between the two families. The negotiation between two families is made by a Raibar (broker). In finalising the marriage both side of the guardian play sole role. The bride or the groom has no choice in this system of marriage. The marriage can take place in the house of bride or groom by concealing both side of the parent. Here all kinds of the matrimonial rites and rituals are observed.

The parents of the boy accompanied by the Raibar go to the girl's house to choose and select her as the bride. If the girl be chosen by the guardian of the boy, then the parents of the girl demand as Daphal and if he did not belong to same Desw, the demand from youth also may be made as per mentioned above. So, among Tripuras, bride did not bring any dowry to her father in law's house. The groom father had to give some price to get wife for his son. Here the dowry system was other way round— the things have changed.

Hamjaklaiwi Kaijakmani (Love Marriage)

Love marriage is very popular in Tripura society traditionally as well in this modern society. When a boy and a girl fall in love with each other and decided to get married, then they bring it to their parent's knowledge. The guardians take initiative if they agree with their child. The procedures of rituals performances in such marriage are same as those in normal social marriages. If the guardian is not agreeing with their children then the marriage did not take place as normal. In this situation they run away from their house and village and get married without their parents' concerned. This type of marriage become elopement marriage as well as love marriage. This type of marriage may be called back to home if their parent want latter on to stay with them, otherwise they have to settle as a separate family.

Twiwi kharlaimani (Elopement Marriage)

In this system of marriage, a boy and a girl who fall in love without the knowledge of their parent usually seek permission from their respective guardian for marriage. However, when their parent did not agree or refused and did not take in sense for arranging their marriage. Then they have no other option except elope in order to fulfil their love, promise and desire. Here the boy play important role and marriage takes place normally by observing all kinds of social rites. The groom has to pay some compensation to the village council if he resettles in the village.

Chamwrwi kamani (Marriage by Service)

Chamwrwi kamani is a process where a bridegroom have to go in-law's house for the fixed tenure carrying along with him kanani-Ri, kamchilik, Da, Daba, Mairang, Thuthai mandwi, etc. (Dhuti, shirt, chopper, Daba, plate, Thuthai mandwi respectively). Some of bridegroom relatives and friends dropped him to 'would be father in law's' house.

The 'would be bridegroom' with his people is welcomed by the bride's family and villagers. On the next day, the groom with his friend and relatives prepared accommodation. After that, groom's relatives and friends go back and groom have to work in would be father in laws house for the fixed period. He does all sorts of works such as huk cutting, sowing, harvesting, and fetching of water, firewood and other works what ever required. He is popularly known as 'Chamwrwi' in the Tripura society.

The groom and bride are not permitted to sleep together till the expiry of period and before ceremonial of marriage conducted by social rites. After the completion of fixed tenure both the guardians will meet and discuss about the marriage. And they have a socially confirmation marriage by obeying all customs in the society. The bridegroom takes bride along with him at his home as a 'Hamchuk'. But at present this system of marriage totally vanished from Tripura community.

Randa/Randi kaijakmani (Widow/Widower marriage)

A widow, widower, and divorcee man and woman are allowed to remarry in the Tripura society. But when a widow or divorcee likes to remarry, she is debarred from observing the rituals which she had once observed in her previous marriage whereas in case of widower it is allowed to observe all kinds of rituals. Both widow and widowers or divorcee have rights to select a bachelor husband and wife as they like. This type of marriage is basically arranged through 'Raibar'. According to observation of W.W. Hunter in his, A Statistical Account of Bengal (p494), " A Tipperah window may remarry, if it so seems good to her. Every lad before marriage has his sweetheart and cohabits with her whenever opportunity serves, this however, is without the knowledge of the elders. I once asked a young man whether he was afraid of his liaison coming to the knowledge of the girls relatives. He replied, "No it is the custom; what can they say? They did the same their young, and their daughter is responsible for own actions. She likes me and I like her."

Forced Marriage

In Tripura community, this is a unique type of marriage in which a girl may be forcefully dragged or carried by the boy and his party. However, the boy who fell in love with that girl should be the first one to touch her. Incase some other person among those group touch her first, then she may choose that person as husband instead of her lover and also if the boy who loved her refuses after the incident then she may choose that person who touch her first. The amount of love may be more or less and even a small gift to a girl is sufficient for this type of marriage.

Divorce

Divorce in the Tripura language known as 'Kaklaimani'. Alike other societies, divorce are in vogue in the Tripura community also. Divorce can be initiated by any one of the spouse. It is either from the husband side or from the wife. The ground of seeking divorce is mainly categorized as under:

1. Mutual incompatibility of temperament.
2. Commission of adultery and unfaithfulness either by the wife or the husband.
3. Carelessness in management of household affairs or habitual neglect of duties and responsibilities.

Tripuras basically depends on their livelihood for farming either through Huk cultivation or wetland cultivation. The division of labour for the husband and wife therefore conforms to the requirement in their daily life. In case the husband is incompetent to shoulder the responsibilities for all works of Huk cultivation or in the field of wetland cultivation i.e., producing of crops, the wife having no alternative seeks divorce from her husband. Similarly in case of mal-adjustment in the domestic affairs, the question of divorce is also taken into consideration.

On the event of commission of adultery and unfaithfulness either by the husband or the wife, seeking of divorce to the Village Council becomes necessary. Moreover, if the husband is addicted to alcohol and torture his wife with the alcoholic influence, the wife can seek divorce to the Village authority.

The proposal for divorce can be initiated either by the husband or wife to the authority of Village Council. For putting up such proposal of divorce, the proposal is to place it in prescribed Rules and Regulation as prevalent in the society. On receipt of the proposal or complaint, the village head convenes a meeting of the Village Council where the seniors and renowned personalities of the village are also invited to attend such meetings. Depending upon the hearing from both sides, the village headman takes decision for such divorce proposal. The decision issued by the village headman is final and is a social binding for both the husband and wife. Divorce which takes place by the decision of the village headman is treated as the final decision of the society.

Since the divorce cases are taken up by the Village Council itself, registration of such cases even does not arise.

In the Tripura Community, judicial divorce is very rare. In other words, the Tripura population prefers to settle such divorce cases within the society itself. Apart from the spouse, divorce can also be sought for by the close relatives either from the husband or from the wife side. Such proposal must be taken with the consent of both the spouses. The close relatives of the spouse also play an active role for consideration in order to avoid divorce.

If the divorcer couple has bear children then it is also announced in the council that with whom they will stay. The minor children either live with their father or the mother as decided by the Village Council. But in case of breast-feeding-baby, the child is always taken in the custody of the mother. For the grown up children they have their option, either to live with the father or the mother after divorce.

In case of divorce for the maintenance of children, if it is vested with the divorced wife, the Village Council also directs to offer maintenance or bear expenditure to the divorced husband. Divorce is also permissible for a woman who is in the family way but in such divorce the husband is under obligation to bear the specific amount of expenditure for the nourishment of post-natal baby.

Divorce is harmful in the life of children in every respect. Among the Tripura, so far divorce is permitted, remarriage is also allowed. But some extend, divorce is not respected in the society and neither encouraged by all.

Kinship System

The kin relationship among Tripura is very familiar. The Tripura men hold highest position in the society as a head of house. The elderly woman enjoys equal respect as the old man in the society of Tripuras. The Tripura Women is equally active and helpful in huk cultivation as well as households except some hard works. The relationship between husband and wife, between children's and parents are very intimate and they have mutual love, affection and interdependence.

Relationship between husband and wife's younger brothers and sisters is very closed and friendly both the sides. But the relation is of distance between son-in-law and parent-in-law and also daughter-in-law, between wife/husband's elder brother and sisters, between wife and husband's uncles. There is a prohibition in some cases between wife and husband's elder brother and uncle. They do not talk each other or neither touches each other. They even can not touch each other's clothes and avoid seeing each other as far as practicable in the society.

Some Kinship Terminologies of the TRIPURAS are:

Terms in English		*Korokborok*
Grand-Father		Chuchu
Grand-Mother		Chwchwi
Father		Bagwi
Mother		Ywgwi
Father-Elder brother]		Yong
Mother-Elder mother	]	
Father-Elder sister	]	Ainchwk
Mother-Elder sister	]	
Father Younger brother		Totoy
Father younger brother wife		Titi
Mother younger brother		Mama
Mother younger brother wife		Nwnwi

Father younger sister	Nwnwi
Father younger sister husband	Mama
Mother younger sister	Titi
Mother younger sister husband	Totoy
Husband	Basai
Wife	Bihik
Father-in-law (Both side)	karaa
Mother-in-law (Both side)	Karachuk
Elder brother	Dada
Sister-in-law(Elder brother's wife)	Bachui
Elder sister	Bwbwi
Brother-in-law(Elder sister's husband)	Kumui.
Brother-in-law(Wife/Husband's Elder brother)	Buwai
Sister-in-law(Wife/Husband's Elder sister)	Waichuk
Sister-in-law (Wife/Husband's younger sister)	Prangchuk
Brother-in-law(Wife/Husband's younger brother)	Prangla
Son	Basachala
Daughter	Basabwrwi
Grand-Son(both male and female)	Sok
Nephew(Younger brother/sister's son)	Baigina
Niece (Younger brother/sister's daughter)	Baiginachuk
Two-sister's husbands	Saruk
Two-brother's wives	Anow
Widow	Randi
Widower	Randa
Adopted Child	Palokmani-basa

Birth Rituals

Pregnancy

When a woman become pregnant the outer surface of the belly gradually become change. Her pregnancy date and months will be counted from her monthly menstruation stops. Generally, from the fifth month of the pregnancy a woman does not co-habit with her husband. It is dangerous for the mother and the baby in the womb. There is no specific restriction on food imposed during the period of pregnancy. At the advanced stage of pregnancy lifting load and doing other hard works is prohibited. It is for the welfare of mother and baby in her womb.

Delivery

When labour pain begins the woman is allowed to lie at the ua Sanal, stretch her legs at Yakathone and let her hand to hold Jawane in a separate room or in a portion of a main room in Tripura custom. For this work two or three Guruma has been engaged and other elder woman from family and neighbourhood. After delivery the new born baby and mother are cleaned with rapid water and are wiped with dry cloth by the Gorwma or other elder woman who are present inside the delivery room. Generally during the delivery only females are allowed to stay inside the delivery room. The males may permit to enter when there arises any great difficulty. At present with the improvement of medical science and availability of doctors and primary health centres, delivery cases are mostly taken to those experts.

Purification

Purification has been done two times to the new born baby in the Tripura society. First purification is done on the day of birth, which is known as 'Abur kisi Sumani'. Without Abur Kisi Sumani the Gurumas are not allowed going home as well as others house. It is believed that without this rite they are impure. They are purified by spreading Kuchai Bwtwi after the Abur Kisi sumani rite. Kuchai Bwtwi is prepared by Silik, Sukui Bwmwtwm, Kuchai Balai, and Tok Thwi. The Abur Kisi Sumani is practiced near the water. This worship is organised by Ochai. The Ochai goes near the river and prepare a Binda by sand, in the middle of Binda he put Mairong chopaha, a pair of *pat* (the leave for *pat* should be barren of flowers and fruits), a piece of *ua-chok* tied with *Khum-Trwng* and a hen or cock as per new born baby male and female respectively. It is believed that by looking intestines of the chicken or cock, they can say good and bad for the new born baby. It is said, right hand side is for god and left hand side is men. So, it is decided accordingly intestine if it is long in the left side the good for the new born baby, otherwise it is favour of god which symbolise bad. The second purification is done after drying of navel. It is also worshiped and practiced same as Abur Kisi Sumani, but it is called as "Abur Karan Sumani".

Name Giving Ceremony

The new born baby name is offered on the seventh day of his/her birth. Name giving ceremony is very found among the Tripura Tribe. They take a plate with some quantity of master oil and arrange all around the plate with Purdy. Purdy is a bunch threads. The people, who are interested in conferring name to the newly born baby, individually select a Purdy in name of their personal choice. When the selection is over, the Purdy burned altogether, the name associated with Purdy that burns to the last is selected for naming the child. But selected Purdy should be always odd number it should not be even number. In this time a small feast is given. The name giving ceremony in the Tripura language is known as 'Bwmwng Bokmani'.

Khalamani (The Ceremony to Feed the New Born Baby)

Khalamani is the richest ceremonial feast observed by Tripuras for new born baby. The Khalamani can be observed three times either five times. There is a rule that the first three times observation of khalamani should be done with Tokla koicha (young cock) and Tokma Koicha (young hen) as per the baby male and female respectively. The special foods and drinks are made for the baby. Food items are *Awan, Toktui, Tokkhan, Mai,* and drinking item is chuwak *pota.* The last two items are done by *uak* (pig); in that time in the food items in place of Tokkhan they give *uakkhan.* This rite is done for the sake of the baby to success in life and to have bright future. The elderly persons blesses to new baby one by one with Khul and Twi spraying the baby. They also offered money and things as a symbol of love and blessing.

Duk Khamani (Worship of Three Gods for the Well Being of New Born Babies)

Duk khamani is a very important rite practised in the birth ritual among Tripuras. The Duk Khamani is a combined worship of three god and goddess; they are Twima, Bikhitra and Darukha. To worship this *matai,* it is required ochai paingthai at the previous night of worship with *patta kaiha* and *khab kaiha.* It is basically worship for the welfare, success and long life of baby. It can be practiced before or after baby born. If it is practiced before birth then as soon as baby become complete fifth months in the mother womb and if it is worship after birth then till he/she attained the age of five years it is permissible to worship. This matai is observed in the deep forest under the tree of Kok-bophang or Jam-bophang or Sallung-bophang (bophang means tree). The tree should be straight and pure with full branches. There should not be any spots, cuts and broken branch on that particular tree. The tree must be bearer of flowers and fruits. Materials required to worship this rite are uak (pig) or Tokhum (duck), Toksa maktham, Dali-khamchi, white thread, wine, etc. The structure is prepared under the tree with bamboo; a house with four poles, place four deep with each of pole, uachok soha, khumtrung, then at the right side Twima and Bikhitra and at the left Darukha with one each *marai, deep, toksa, potta, path,* etc. After that the Ochai mantra sawi sacrified the *uak* or *Takhum* and then the *Toksa* for each one Twima,

Bikhitra and Darukha. Ochai tied the tree and the poles together with white thread by mantra seventh times as ayuk sousa-w, at the time father has to hold thread. It is believed that father need to cut five or three times to that particular tree at that time. Otherwise, the particular family can not take the tree, even if they are in need.

All the material whatever is used in the worship is not allowed to bring at home, except one Toksa which is scarified at the Darukha. Other all eatable things are needed to have at the spot itself. Darukha Toksa is brought at home as an Ayuk phola. The Ayuk-phola need to give the particular baby, if baby is in the womb then to the mother. The Ochai ask to baby parent, *"Nini cherokni ayukphola mandwi manha"*. The parent of the baby needed to reply, *"Manha"*. Sema swngmani, the parents of child asked to Ochai by offering one bottle wine bowing down head to his leg, *"Par-pur rok gamdwi, Toksa ramani rok gamdwi"*. The Ochai needed to reply, *"Gam-se"*. At last the Ochai tied bithi with white thread at the five place hands, legs and neck and bless for successful life.

Influence of the globalisation leads people to make flexible every thing. People continuously converted since last few decade, in their life style and religion. As 'human wants are never end', people always search for comfortable life and society. Even lots of Tripuras converted their title from Tripura to Debbarmas, Reangs, Noatia, Jamatias, etc. some by willingly and some by bound where nearby they inhabited as 'Panji habw'. In the socio-customs they change from Animism to Hinduism or Christianity. Peoples of this day hardly practice the above cited rites. In place of that they dedicated to church and celebrated as birth day of the new born baby. The name of the new born baby is selected in the church or selected by their parent directly.

Death Rituals

The Tripura tribe cremates the corpse on the next day.

They observe certain practices surrounding the dead body like other aboriginals. They make chariot and the corpse is placed on it, after that they pulls the chariot to the burning ground. A son of the deceased or older mans sets fire to the corpse by lighting straw. The procedures are as follows:

When a death occurs in a Tripura family, the relatives and neighbours are informed first by the family members of the deceased person. At first they will prepare a Songbai Nok to keep the death body. The Songbai nok is prepared by six piece of Thong (Bamboo poles), four piece of Lagara, and a number of bamboo splits are placed crosswise on the thong and lagara then are tied them with ropes. Six piece of Mwikhun bathai prepared by Risa has to be tied in the Songbai nok. It is covered in the top as roof with white cloth. Then they give bath the dead body with boil water and dress it up. The dead body keep laid at Songbai nok. The dead body of the head is directed towards North. A cock is killed at the feet of the dead body by striking it on the ground with the left hand. Rice is cooked in the Wasung (bamboo pipe) or in the pot. The cooked rice and chicken is offered on the feet of the dead body with Maikhalai made of banana leaf having four corners on the Maicham made of bamboo. Near the Maicham they keep a pair of Kaichok, two piece of thola, a pair of pat and Khap with water for washing hand. It is for longmatai and dead man, as eating together by washing their hand. The leg side of the dead body a Yapriha/Thilaha of white thread is placed. Thereafter, they play drum as symbol of death, there is a theme and particular beat of drumming in Tripura Tribe by which people can recognise that some one died. The relatives and other persons who come to pay homage to the dead body give paddy, cotton, sesame, coin, etc. at the feet of the dead body.

On the next day early in the morning the relatives, neighbours and villagers engage in different works. They were divided in groups for the preparation of Tolai, Mangchong and chariot or Kerang Kholang or latha (any one of them is necessary). The Tolai (bier) of the dead body is made of bamboo. Two bamboo poles eight to ten feet in length are placed parallel to each other. A number of bamboo splits are placed crosswise on the two poles and tied to them with ropes. Red and black thread is tied to the four sides of the poles. After observing certain social practices the dead body is taken out from Songbai and shifted to Tolai. It is a carrier of dead body from home to cremation place. Generally the adult sons, son-in-laws, nephews and in absence of them the family friends of the deceased lift the Tolai up on their shoulders uttering 'Hari Hari Bol' three times and start for the cremation ground. A person carries the Nokhai containing the paddy, cotton, sesame, chopper, coin and Yapriha/Thilaha white of thread pulling like channel from hoe to funeral ground and sprinkled other articles contained in the Nokhai on the road ahead of the procession. After reaching in the cremation ground the Tolai carrier of dead body keep the ground in a manner that the head of the dead body directs towards the north. Now they purchase land for the deceased at the rate of Pasiga (1.25 paise) and one bottle wine at the place where Mangchong was prepared. But at present the rate increased from Pasiga to five rupee and one bottle that are compulsory now and earlier.

Chariot or Kerang Kholang or latha or Along any one of them is needed in the process of cremation in the dead rituals of Tripuras. This practice is done in the cremation ground before placing dead body in to the Mangchong. The Rot (Chariot) is prepared by bamboos, 4 wheels, 4 Yamaduk Buduk and the deceased party needed to buy it from those who prepared it by 5 rupees and one bottle wine. Next to rot is Kerang Kholang, Latha or Along, it is without wheels and Buduk.

The Mangchong is prepared at the place of cremation

with wood and bamboo. The Mangchong is prepared in the direction of North-South pole. Two bamboo poles are planted in the western side, one by the leg and other one by the head. Similarly two bamboos are planted in the eastern side also. After that if it is male decease then three stag of wood and two stag of dry bamboo and if it is female then five stag of wood and one stag of dry bamboo is necessary to keep in the Mangchong. After the dead body is placed on the firewood again some firewood are placed on the dead body. A piece of new cloth equal to the length of the body is to be hung over the dead body and different colour of Risa is also hung.

Lighting fire—The elder son or youngest son of the deceased person has a right of lighting fire. In absence of sons eldest person present at the place of cremation Lights fire. Before lighting fire they practice some social custom around the Mangchong. Then they set fire a bunch of bamboo stick and stand two people one in west side and other in east. They will touch the bunch of fire leg side and head three or five or seven times. After that they will make fire first at the cloth hung over the dead body. Number of people present in the cremation ground has been counted by collecting Gwnti (a piece of wood). As soon as fire is set, people start moving from cremation ground but some remain till the end. The woman participants offered wine, that wine is drunk by those who remain there till the end of burning. All the participants of the cremation return to deceased house after taking bath in the nearby water sources and they take sanctified water of Tulsi leaf on their head and sake fire as purification. While coming from cremation ground looking back is strictly prohibited for everybody.

On the next day of cremation family members of the deceased, relatives and some eldest man and woman goes to the cremation ground to collect bones of the dead. They offer cooked rice, curry, wine, water, etc. to deceased by observing Lampra Uathwp worship. In the cremation ground they set free a chicken in the name of deceased. After observing all the rites they bring the bones putting in the bamboo pipe and keep hung some where in the corner of house. This rite is known among the Tripura Tribe as 'Kereng Thum Mani'. This bones is poured in the holy place like Gumuti river, Ganga, Brahmaputra, etc. as Kereng Khwi-w for the departed soul of deceased. But for this rite there is no time and period bounded, at any time whenever party can do. After observing this rite they need to feed people in the name of deceased.

Mourning Period

Duration of mourning period may be seven days, thirteen days, but maximum people observed on the next day of cremation. This ceremony is called in Tripuras 'Kwthwi Mairw-w'. In the mourning period the restriction and prohibition among Tripuras are cutting hair, nail, shave beard, moustache and taking fish, meat, dry fish, Rotten fish, etc. On the day of Kwthwi Mairwmani the male members of the deceased family shave off hair, moustache and cut nails. To observe the ceremony they need to cut a pig or buffalo and prepare a NOK SAR in the cremation ground facing towards east if deceased is male and for female facing towards west. They prepared foods for deceased, if they cut pig, then *singmol bakhan phwntham, panjara bakhan phwntham, bwlwk, Khachok phwntham, yaphwng phwntham, Yaitam kaiha, bukung, bwmwtwm, salai, khunjur,* and egg boil, rice *(prengjak),* wine as Achar. They take it to cremation ground in the Nok sar and offer food and drinks to departed soul. The relatives and other who participates there take part as pat nai-w and twi, chuwak ser-ow. They host in the cremation ground chekhara maitang with bamboo and Chin with bamboo poles Risa. During this ceremony they organised a feast. Death rituals ended with the rites of Khumbokwi in the middle month of March and beginning of April.

In case of victims of Cholera, Small pox, Leprosy and Tuberculosis the corpse are disposed off by burial. Again in case of dead within a month of the newly born baby, is placed in a cradle and hung in a big tree in the dense forest. But now-a-days this custom is not in vogue at all.

Devotional Practices of Tripuras

The Tripura tribe has good number of popular god and goddesses. The deities have great influence on their mental life. Among the deities some are taken to be benevolent while some are to be malevolent. The malevolent deities or spirits are held to wreak havoc to both mental and physical life. For that Tripuras are very careful to appease the hostile by the way of sacrificing animals and birds. The gods and goddesses of the Tripuras have no concretised visual symbols of abstract concept or no ideas for each one of which there is mental vision. Therefore the abstract symbols of the natural deities are made with the helps of bamboo poles, bamboo leaves and cotton thread etc. the bamboo made structure of a deity to some extent may be called an alter or a pedestal of the deity, but if we identify it as the abode of deity "Matai-nok", surely, this will also be justified. Among the Tripuras traditional symbols of the deities are made in a peculiar way instructed by the Ochai who has to follow the specific designs at the time of constructing the certain deity. The number and shape of the bamboo poles vary from one structure to another.

The bamboo worship was not only earliest form of divine ritual, but it was existed long before the creation of temple and images of the gods and goddesses. But one should notice that only the green-bamboo is regarded as sacred. The dry bamboo is deprived of all its sacred nature.

In Tripuras each gods and goddesses has a qualifying term of address as "Ma" and "pha" which means

"Mother" and "Father' respectively. It is good to remind ourselves that the sea, the sky and the mountain seem to be the gods and the earth, the water and the tree become the goddess and so on. The Tripuras worship them in different places with different names by ochai or without ochai offering Dali-Khamchi, Chuak Kathar and domestic animals like goats, chickens, pigs, etc.

The following are the deities of their own :

Benevolent Deities

1. **Matai Gorja**, *(Matai=God; Gorja=chief).*

Matai Gorja is supreme god believed by the Tripuras. It is parallel to Lord Siva of Hindu.

2. **Twima/Twibukma** *(Twi=Water; Ma= Goddess).*

Twima is a Goddess of water, parallel to the Gangas of Hindu pantheon.

3. **Mainungma** *(Mai=paddy; Ma= Goddess).*

Mainungma is a goddess of fortune, wealth and prosperity, parallel to Goddess Laxmi of Hindu.

4. **Khunungma** *(Khul=Cotton ; Ma=Goddess)*

It is a goddess of cotton.

5. **Hachukma** *(Hachuk =Mountai; Ma =Goddess).*

It is a Goddess of hills and mountains, parallel to the Parboti, consort of Lord Siva, and resident of Kailash mountain of Himalayas.

6. **Noksub matai**. It is a household deity.

7. **Kalia bai Goria** : God of agriculture and crops.

Kalia and Goria are two brothers. Goria deity is more prominent and worshipped as the god of crops and good harvest in the huk and wetland cultivation. Goria dance is performed during Buisu festival in the month of April. But when the gods are worshipped jointly it is called 'Bonerok'.

8. **Lampra Uathob**: God of sky, path and sea. It is worshipped for the well-being of the self as well as society.

9. **Sakni Matai** : God of health. It is also a household deity. It protects the family members from the evil eye of the evil spirits.

10. **Parakermani (A kind of worship to drive out the evil spirits from the village)**: It is presided by individual hamlet and community life of mass people. It is performed to ride out the evil spirits from the villages. It is performed either on Tuesday or Saturday. It is performed within fortified area. Nobody is allowed to go out or enter during the performance of matai for the period of one day and one night. Absolute serenity and solitude are a must to be maintained for the matai. It brings well-being and prosperity for the whole village.

Malevolent Deities

1. **Brwisni**: The seven witches are called Brwisni. It is believed that among the sisters the youngest is unmarried and prone to do harm to human beings.

2. **Burasa**: A male deity held by Tripuras to cause various diseases to human being. Hence is to be propitiated with offering fowls and eggs.

3. **Sakal** : A deity of witches. To get rid off from the attack of any diseases, Sakal is to be propitiated.

4. **Bonerok**: A group of evil deity who cause harm to the human.

Some explanation of how Tripuras worshipped their gods and goddesses :

Lampra Uathwb (A kind of worship on road to invoke good fortune, before embarking upon any thing new):

Lampra Uathob is an important religious rite practised by Tripuras. Lampra is the combination of two korokborok terms, 'Lam' and 'pra' which means Road or path and the joining or crossing branches of the roads respectively. The 'Uathob' literally means clump of bamboo. It is worship on the mouth of two or more road merged as to make clear and save throughout the ways they goes or their works from evil spirits and other unwanted things. The social activities and religious practices of Tripura Tribe begin with the lampra uathob. It is basically worshiped for three occasion *lamakachal thangphu-w, Sakni bawi, Kathar samung khalai-ani, Sakang (huk wak-ani sakang, Kailai-ani sakang* etc.). The name of god which is worship in the lampra uathob is Sukundra and Mukundra. Sukundra and Mukundra are two brothers. They are worshiped before any auspicious work to drive away the evil spirits from the path.

To make the structure of the deities, two pairs of bamboo poles measuring 50 to 65 cm in height are planted in the ground on the court-yard. Afterwards, two other bamboo poles are tied to these planted bamboo poles horizontally. On the bamboo planted in the ground on that courtyard they planted three deep in each poles and one on the middle. It appears that the bamboo poles are the symbolic representations of the deities. This bamboo poles structure which altogether became uathob is fully prove in the presence of the supernatural deities and spirits among the Tripura Tribe. In any case, we have no ground to believe the idea of full standing image prevailing among the Tripuras during the ancient period. The real fact is that the bamboo itself is worshipped in its natural form and the deities of Tripuras are not personified and endowed with human shape. As the object of the ritual the bamboo made *Uathob* is needed in every matai of the Tripuras after some addition or alteration regarding sizes and decorative works around the bamboo poles in the times of making it any items. E. T. Dalton remarks that, " a trace of their old faith is to be found in their present religious festival and worshipping it."

Similar to Tripuras "the Garos and Kacharis sacrifice

before a bamboo planted in the ground. The Bihors worship their godling 'Darha' in the form of split bamboo, Mraris make the pair at marriage nok round a bamboo in a bamboo shed and ascetic Sanyasi should carry a bamboo staff with knots."(William Crooke, *Religion and Folklore of Northern India,* p. 414).

Let us come to our point, the Tripuras have the priest who is called Ochai. The Ochai always conducts the 'Lampra matai' and the symbolic bamboo made uathob is also constructed by him and his helper. The ingredients of the matai consist of banana leaves, two cock, bamboo water pipe, cotton, wine, rice, *khultrung,* etc. When every thing is in order, the Ochai kneels on the ground and starts the matai. Chanting the mantras and sprinkling the water from bamboo pipe the Ochai begins matai. Afterwards, two cocks are scarified and their blood is dedicated to the deities on undried rice which is kept in the banana leaf in front of uathob. The Ochai does not completely sever the neck of the cocks. Cutting the half portion of the neck of the cocks the Ochai offers the blood to the deities. After that the cock is completely beheaded. As soon as the sacrifice is over the Ochai sprinkles water and wine over the head of the cocks. It is a fact that in case of leaser deities, the neck of the scarified animal is half cut, but in case of higher deities, the neck of the animal has to be completely severed.

The Ochai forecast whether the deities are satisfied with the worshipper or not by tossing pat. He takes two leaves in his hand and tosses them in the air in front of the uathob. It is believed, if one falls flat on the ground, another fall back on the ground, it is good sign. Thus from the reading of the pat is declared that the deities have pleased with devotees and they will do well to the families. When reading is auspicious the ochai will order the devotee to sacrifice two cocks in the name of the deities so that they may be pleased.

Mainungma Matai (A Post Harvestment Worship)

The Tripuras have to be said the worshipper of natural forces as the Gods and Goddesses like the other tribal communities of the North-east India. The Mainungma is worshiped as the mother Goddess of earth and giver of blessing for increasing the productivity of paddy and crops. The mainungma is commonly known as the Goddess of paddy. In the mainungma matai Tripuras also worshiped jointly her husband Khulnung and the daughter Lwkkhi. The Khulnung God mixed with earth who is worshiped for abundant supply of cotton crops and the Lwkkhi for guard and shape of storing paddy and other crops. Tripuras generally worshiped Mainungma matai for the "Maichok khulchok bangrwani bagwi".

The Mainungma Matai is worship by Ochai and his assistant Tanchorai. It is worship in the paddy field or huk. The symbolic representation of these deities is prepared at the bottom of paddy plants. The marai designs made of bamboo are planted at the bottom of paddy plant 11 sticks for *Mainungma* in the middle, 5 sticks for khulnung at the left side of *Mainungma* and 9 sticks for Lwkkhi at the right side of *Mainungma*. One each Maicham with Maikhalai is placed in front of them. Ingredients placed in the *maikhalai* are rice, *awan* (11 nos, 5nos, and 9 nos respectively), Mairong chopaha, laijorha, potta kongha, pat jorha, egg and she-pig for mainungma, tokla for khulnung and tok for the lokhi. When the arrangement is over the ochai begins worship by mantra *patewi* (chanting mantra) and tosses pat by holding the leaves in his finger and throwing in the air in front of deity's structure for each of them. It is believed, if one falls flat on the ground, another fall back on the ground, it is good sign. Thus from the reading of the pat is declared that the deities have pleased with devotees and they will be good for them. When reading is auspicious the ochai asked his assistant tanchorai to scarified she-pig first then *tokla* and *tok* respectively for *mainungma,* khulnung and lwkkhi. After sacrificing the animals first session come to end.

They take pig *biyak yakha* and head of scarified pig, and both chickens for *achar*. They make curry with pig head and boil chickens. The ochai once again begins his worship for second session as *achar nai-w* by placing all the boil items and cook curry as accordingly. After *achar naimani* is over the owner collects all things in the kalbang except she-pig head curry. The curry is distributed among the members present there and eaten there itself as *khuk musur-w*. After that they walk for home, the owner lady carry *kalbang* and hold tirkong walk at first. The owner invites all villagers and relatives for the feast in the name of mainungma in the particular day.

Twima Matai (Worship in Water)

The Twima Matai is identified with a major forces of nature; the Water. The nature deity Twima matai as a water goddess performs her defined role and ensures her protection to her worshipper. The Twima matai is worshiped in according to Tribal custom as to precautionary measure against the disease, protection of the self, child, family and villages from the danger of water goddess: the Twima and also worshiped for the welfare of the fields productivity and fertility. The goddess Twima is said to have control over the water. It is believed that if her satisfaction is made by paying reverence to them, the whole supernatural of river's water will not do any evil to human society. The supernatural power who resides the river's water was identified as mother goddess Twima. The Tripuras consider that the worship of Twima will make the life substantial and there will be no scarcity of water.

Procedures observed by Tripuras to worship Twima matai is Ochai thwlw at the previous night of the Twima matai. The Ochai and his assistant Tanchorai are asked for performing matai by the owner. The Ochai and his assistant Tanchorai will sit in the *khola* together.

The materials are chopper, lai jornwi and twilota thaiha. The Ochai begins with sprinkling water to leaf by chanting mantra and cut the leaf seven times upward and downward both of them Ochai and his assistant Tanchorai. Then Owner is asked to watch dream in the night.

In the day of Twima matai, early in the morning they prepared ingredients like twisikong design of marai made downward four times and two times upward, dali-khamchi, mairong mochom, goat, chicken, banana leaf, etc. On the river four bamboo poles are planted the heads of which are rising on the surface of water in a small squares areas, the four bamboo poles are tied together with the help of another four pieces of bamboo poles. In the middle of this structure a platform (Machang) is constructed. On the surface of platform a banana leaf is placed and other ingredients are placed on the banana leaf and goat and chicken are kept near the deity. After that the Ochai begins matai by chanting mantra holding Twisikong in the right hand and sprinkling water, dali-khamchi. The ochai tosses pat by holding the leaves in his finger and throwing in the air in front of deity's structure for each of them. It is believed, if one falls flat on the ground, another fall back on the ground, it is good sign. Thus from the reading of the pat is declares that the deities have pleased with devotees and they will good for them. When reading is auspicious the ochai asked his assistant tanchorai to sacrify chicken first and then goat. It is believed that by looking intestines of the chicken they can say whether the Twima Goddess is satisfied or not with scarifice made upon her name. It is said, right hand side is for goddess and left hand side is for worshipper. So, it is decided accordingly intestine if it is long in the left side then the Twima goddess is satisfied with worshipper; otherwise it is in favour of Goddess, it means she is not satisfied with worshipper and their scarified. At the end all members those who are present in the worshiping spot apply gabi on the forehead as goat-tale.

Burasa Matai (Worship of Evil Spirits of Forest God)

Burasa is supernatural spirit of the forest who always looks after the welfare of its inmates and malevolent in character. In the Burasa matai, there is certainly an element of fear and it is confirmed that he stands for diseases. The Tripuras believe that the severe pain diseases of a child or fever are caused by the deity Burasa. The Burasa Matai is rendered so that the patient may be cured by blessings of the supernatural spirit. The Burasa Matai is observed by Ochai in the deep part of the forest. The Matai may be held in day light or in sylvan semidarkness of evening. The Ochai is accompanied by the male members of the family. The woman and children are not allowed to visit the place of Matai. A bamboo made uathub is needed for the ritual practised. In this matai the Ochai scarified she-pig or duck to make satisfied Burasa. Thereafter, the head of the animal, pieces of nalls of the sacrificed animal, pieces of meat, pieces of wings and entrails are given to the deity along with the wine of bottle. The matai is rounded off with a feast in which the entire members present in the place of matai itself. The sacrificed animal meat is not allowed to bring home or village from the forest.

3

Health Profile of Tripuras

Folk Medicine Practised by the Tripuras

Physical ailment is vital problem for human society, primitive or advanced, and every society has evolved its own method of treatment to cure an ailment. The Tripuras minds disease as a matter of great mental concern and feel a lot of anxiety about them. They scare the disease but at the same time have mentality to fight against. The human society which is still in the primitive stage resorts to treat the diseases with aid of herbal plants and magic. The use of herbal plants to tie over frequent diseases is universally taken to by entire human society all over the world. This system is scientific though not done rationally due to inadequate knowledge about application.

Whenever a person suffers from a disease, the first thing that comes to his mind is to know the cause of the disease. When they have identified the disease, first of all they used herbal plant as must as they know to cure disease. If disease is not cured at a time then they call Ochai. The Ochai resorts to treatment of any disease by combining magic and herbal plants which goes hand in hand in the application of medicines and incantations. They hold that, application of medicine alone can not cure diseases unless magic or mantra is enchanted. Therefore Ochai is established as right person to handle method of treatment. Ochai is not only a priest to perform worship but also physician to handle the diseases.

Methods of Treatment

The methods and system of treatments used by the Tripuras for the ailments can be classified into the following categories;

House-Hold Treatment

In case of ordinary diseases or at the first stage of any disease, a patient is treated by some old and experienced members of his family.

Treatment by the Ochai (Priest/Ojha)

When the disease goes beyond the range of house-hold treatment then the village Ochais treatment is required. If the village Ochai fails to cure, the patient take help of a famous Ochai from other village.

The mode of Ochai treatment varies from patient to patient as per the nature of diseases. The Ochai conducts the treatment through the following methods:

a. Divination to ascertain the cause of the disease,

b. The use of medicine prepared from various roots and herbs,

c. The distribution of amulets and sanctified water,

d. The worship and propitiation of the aggrieved spirit, and

e. The neutralisation of the affect of an evil eye etc.

Divination is the chief weapon of an Ochai to cure a patient. Through divination, he ascertains the evil spirits or the aggrieved deity responsible for disease and tries to cure the patient through propitiation of it. The method of divination used by the Ochai is very interesting. The Ochai first of all finds out the identity of the aggrieved deity or sakal that is to be propitiated to neutralise the disease. This method is called Thikana Naimani (finding out the identity). The Ochai recognise the aggrieved sakal causing the disease by the process of thikana naimani.

Then in the next stage Sema Naimani, in which the ochai tells what should be done for the cure. Then the Ochai performs the required Matai (Puja), after the matai he tells the result of it, which is known as Sema Samani. The term Sema means result. In the sema samani, the Ochai explain whether the deity is satisfied with his worship and the disease is curable or not. If the disease is out of his jurisdiction he advice for another better Ochai. They believe only the Ochai is competent medicine man to bring relief to a patient due to the aggressive intention of another Ochai.

Ochai's treatment constitutes an important element of sacrificing of goats, fowls, eggs, ducks etc. During the times of thikana naimani the Ochai comes to know the kind of the animal to be sacrificed. The burasa likes chicken, eggs, ducks etc. and the sakal prefers goats, pig etc. The worship may be simply performed by offering a dali-kamchi if the spirit wished it.

In some case the Ochai gives amulets to the patient for wearing on arms, neck, and waist to ward off the evil eye. Restrictions on diets are also prescribed by the Ochai according to the nature of the disease.

Faith Healing

Faith healing plays a very important role in the Tripura community. The practice of promising an animal e.g. goat, pig, fowls etc. and different mantras and tantras and also matai. Motivation of all religious functions is seeking for the protection of the natural forces and evil spirits from the attack of diseases, famine, and flood and crop destruction.

Now-a-days, due to globalised development, modern allopathic medicines for ordinary common diseases are available in most of the village markets. So, any delay in curing of a patient in their traditional system of treatment he/she takes allopathic medicine from the market or goes to quack. But if this medicine also fails to cure patient, then the patient is taken to the hospital. In case of failure of hospital treatment, the patient is taken back home and the treatment of the Ochai is solicited. There are many cases where doctor would not cure but cured by Ochai.

The Ochai are not paid any fees as such in cash for his services. He is given a meal and a drink of chuwak. But at present the cost of ingredients for a matai has become very high. The helpers of the Ochai who are known as Baruas are also given meals. It is mentioned that any person can be taken as Barua or Tanchorai. Tanchorai is taken only in case of sacrifice of animal is made at matai. He is just a helper and need not know any mantra.

Diseases – uses of plants and herbs – their management and treatment

Kongrai (Catarrh)

The Tripuras name for catarrh is kongrai. The medicine man of Tripuras divides catarrh into three types as per season of occurrence. These are –

a. Saltung kongrai (the summer cold),.

b. Uatwi kongrai (the rain cold), and

c. Masing Kongrai (the winter cold).

Sneezing and coughing are the main symptoms of this disease.

The composition of the medicine for the catarrh is

mwkhwrwi sechuwa (a kind of thorny plant) and *thendoroi* with an amount of salt and green chilly. These substances are put together into a bamboo pipe and grounded into paste with the help of bamboo pestle. Then the mouth of pipe is closed with a cork and put on fire to be heated. This hot substance is taken by the patient three to four times a day. It gives relief from the cold. By this system of treatment discharge from the nose dries up quickly.

Another effective medicine for the cold and fever used by the Tripuras is Chakhrwi bwtwi (Alkali water). This is taken lukewarmly. It stops sneezing. Some times the paste of silik bwtwi (green turmeric) is added to this water.

In case of little children, warm water and hot rice are recommended. In addition to it, they are protected from external cold and are also not allowed to eat and drink cold food.

Kuchu-ma (Cough)

The *kuchu-ma* is generally divided into three types and they are:

a. kongrai-ni-kuchuma (hawking cough),

b. Hulok (hoping cough), and

c. kash (Asthma).

Generally, in Tripura community kongrai-ni-kuchuma patient is given treatment with the warm juice of the young white leaves of the pineapple plant.

The juice of *sichuwa balai* (the leaf of a kind of thorny plant which is occasionally used as fencing of the house) is also a very good medicine for this disease.

The young leaves of Mwilok (white gourd) and some tamarinds are heated in bamboo pipe and this hot substance is given to the patient.

It should be noted that sweet is strictly vetoed in case of cough and cold.

Kulum (Fever)

Fever in term of Tripura language known as Kulum. The temperature of a patient is felt by touching their wrist, forehead or body.

In case of very high temperature a special method of treatment is applied to bring it down. The root of kwicherma plant is paste and filtered with a piece of cloth. The filtrate is mixed with the water. The head and body of a patient is sponged with mixed water.

The patient is also given the juice of a creeper named 'Dobayei'. In fact it is worth mentioning here Berema consider as an effective medicine and preventive of malaria. Malaria is the most common disease in their locality. When a person feels feverish, he at once takes some Berema mixed with water. Thus berema may be termed as the quinine.

In case of severe headache the astringent juice of seedy banana or the juice of gourd leaf is applied on the forehead. Some times mild taps are given on the affected part.

Pwrjal Balumbowa (All Kinds of Bee Sting)

In case of bee sting, the stings are first taken out and then a little amount of honey is rubbed on the affected area. In case of excessive pain, the afflicted person is given a hot bath. The mixture of treacle (Kwtwra) and lime is also applied on the wound.

Chibuk Sukmani (Snake Bitting)

The treatment of snake bite is also done by the Ochai through charms and incantations. Generally, the upper portion of the affected place is tied with a rope very tightly to stop blood circulation of that place.

Mangtai (Diarrhoea)

It is believe that once a person is attacked by Mangtai, he will be attacked by it again about the same time the following year. The symptom of Mangtai is like that of cholera. The only difference is that Mangtai is not an infectious disease as per them.

In this disease, the patient is exposed to sufficient light and air. The bark of chethuwang (Alstenia xchelaris) tree is grounded into a paste and it is soaked in water for a while. This water is given to patient. It stops the vomiting tendency and motion immediately.

Beside the above mentioned medicine the patient is also given a mixture of Toksa kwlwi and silik kwthwng (green Turmeric). Toksa kwlwi in a sense that the chicken just been hutched and not touched the earth yet. The chicken is boiled with green turmeric in a bamboo pipe.

Hor-khammani (Burn)

The burn place should not be touched and application of water to it is restricted. The astringent juice Sapai Balai (been leaf) mixed with an amount of Swm (salt) is applied to the affected area. The mixture of Chundwi Bwtwi (lime water) and Narke thok (coconut oil) is also applied. The cold mud collected from the place where the earthen pitcher is also applied to relieve the burning sensation.

Mwksa (Eye Disease)

When pain cause in the eye, a few lemons leaved are boiled in water and applied to the eye. The hot compression of boiled rice is also used. The breast milk of the mother of a sucking baby is also considered as an effective medicine. It is dropped in the effected eye.

Beside, to cure the minor ophthalmic the chewed onion is sprinkled on the eye. The person who treats chews one or two whole onion in the mouth forcefully on the effected eye or eyes. This method is proved to be effective.

Rwbwm (Swelling)

In case of swelling of any part of the body a chuwan tablet is made into a paste with hot water and the paste is applied on the attached place.

The Chuwan is used as an ingredient to prepare rice beer. This is composition of the leaf chamatwi tree, gabi, jackfruit leaf, garlic, chilly, ginger, etc. All this materials are grounded into powder mixed with water and prepared into tablets. It is an effective medicine.

Sak-Mechermani (Urinary Disease)

In case of urinary diseases like feeling of burning sensation at the time of passing frequent urination, the seeds of the Takhurung plant are kept soaked in water for an hour. The mixture is given to patient.

Gamasi (Prickly Heat of Summer)

The Gamasi is cure with the application of rain water. The rubbing of baati Bumuthu (the piece of cloth which is used for filtering the wine) on the body also reduces the prickly heat of the summer.

Khiw-kaba-w (Cholara)

In Tripura term cholera is called Khiw-kabaw. It is like pox which is considered to break out from the wrath of Kalia. The Ochai is the chief medicine man of this disease and he gives khulom (sanctified thread) to all the villagers. The paramudra (sanctified of the para) is also done in addition to the matai of kalia.

The dead body in this case, is cremated immediately.

Ok Samani (Stomach Pain):

Severe stomach pain is given special type of treatment. The rubbing of mustard oil on the effected part some time reduces the pain for the time being. But permanent relief can be obtained by Omathai-khamani.

Kasa/Tanjakmani (Cuts):

In case of injury or cut by any things, the bleeding is stopped by application of charms and incantations by the Ochai. Beside that the juice of the leaf of Mai-sundwi, Tulsi, and Durba is used for stopping bleeding.

Beside, the above mentioned the following are the methods of treatment with the aid of plants and creepers adopted by Tripuras :

1. If any body suffers from loss of appetite the crushed seed of 'Tharai' with water is given to take. Tharai is a kind of soft plant grown on the low and marshy land.
2. To cure the ulcer in the backside of a child's ear the ashes of 'Muikhumu' (Mushroom), is applied in the affected area.
3. A sore caused by burn is treated by a mixture prepared from coconut oil and limewater.
4. In case of eruption on the facial part of a person they apply a paste prepared from the baked solid collected from the earthen oven.
5. In case of vomiting tendency, indigestion and constipation the patient is given to take the baked salt.
6. A child suffering from cold is given to take honey for remedy.
7. A patient suffering from pain while passing out urine or insufficient outflow of urine is given to take the seed of Tukuma plant. The seed is

dissolved in the water and it gets swelled up. The patient is given to take it.

Treatment of Bone-Fracture

Both compound and simple bone fractures can be treated well by some Tripuras Bwidya who collects leaves and barks of particular medicinal plants which are not known by the common people. The leaves and barks of the medicinal plants firstly are collected from jungle and reducing the mixed ingredients to paste they apply the paste mixed up with yolk in the broken part of the limbs. The process of plastering by the modern way of orthopaedic treatment is followed by them. The broken part is tightly fastened by the cloth and to keep the affected part straight and erect (in case of leg and hand) they bind the pasted part with bamboo-sticks around. It is as good as hard-plaster by the modern treatment.

4

Economic Profile of Tripura Tribe: Traditional to Modern Life

The Tripuras are mainly an agriculturist Tribe and agriculture is the main source of their livelihood and economics assistants. All the members of the family work for production, but division of labour is made according to sex and age. The boys and girls are allotted different jobs suited to their age. The woman folk play an important role in their agricultural work and also the economics support. Besides the agricultural work, a small number of them are also engaged in the some other types of work like house construction, trade and commerce, transport and communication, but they are directly or indirectly linked with the agriculture. The principal traditional economics activities of Tripura Tribe are vested on Huk, which literally means shifting cultivation and forest products. They are traditionally cultivators and dwellers of the forest. The forest is the main source of their economy.

The Tripuras earned their livelihood by food gathering, food producing, domesticating animal, cottage industry etc. surrounding where they inhabited. As a natural process, the food-gathering activities of the Tripuras are supplement by the primitive method of agriculture as Huk cultivation or shifting cultivation. So, at a time they are economically self-contained and self-sufficient. They make their own articles of daily use as their requirements without any help from extraneous source. But at present, money economy has changed the nature and character of the economic life pattern of Tripura Tribe. They also become prone to outside cultural influences. This becomes balance less economy in the society. This would be evident from the sources of historical and empirical of the economic activities of the Tripuras under such heading as: huk cultivation, plough or wetland cultivation, food-gathering, food production, handicrafts, weaving, daily labour, animal husbandry, employment, etc.

Huk Cultivation (Shifting Cultivation)

Until the recent past, huk cultivation was the integral part of tribal life and economic in Tripura State. This primitive method of agriculture was directly associated with the dawn of human civilization Shifting cultivation undoubtedly, the next state of transformation of human life from the cave dwellers, depending upon livelihood on hunting, fishing in the stone-age. The Tripura communities of Tripura have been practising huk cultivation from time immemorial and through centuries together. The individual, the family and social life of the Tripuras were directly associated and controlled by this primitive agricultural practice.

Even up to the first half of twentieth century, the Tripura communities by and large had been enjoying a peaceful life without much hindrance as Huk cultivation, had been able to provide them with almost all supports of their livelihood excepting some of the essential goods such as salt, dry fish, molasses etc. Those items they used to collect from the far-flung markets in the plain areas within the State and Commilla, Bala Bazar etc. in the erstwhile Tipperah District adjacent to Hill Tipperah.

The huk cultivator society and their life cycle were totally dependent upon this cultivation. Birth, Death, social rituals, music, dance, weaving, handicrafts, ornaments whatever the requirement of human life were derived from huk and forest resources.

The main source of income of Tripuras is cultivation. Huk is their original source of income since long past. Traditionally, the Tripuras are vested on the Huk cultivation. But till today a good number of the Tripuras tribe are practising Huk cultivation in a limited scale. The Huk cultivation literally means shifting cultivation. To make completed operation of Huk cultivation they need to observe eight stages. This may be noted as follows: i) Selection of the Huk-field and its rituals, ii) Cutting and Tools used in Huk operations, iii) Burning and preparation of the field, iv) Sowing of seeds, v) Weeding and sprouting, vi) Protection of Huk, vii) Harvesting, and viii) Threshing and storing.

First of all the land is selected in the hill range, Hillocks and slopes with forest cover as Huk Nai-w. It is basically selected during the month of November and December. They always select a virgin site bearing bamboos and bushes and making all sorts of provision for the protection of the crops. The selection is fixed in accordance dreams of the head of the family. If he dreams fish, cock, etc, than it is considered to be good for Huk cultivation. On the other hand, if he dreams water, dying domestic animals, etc, are considered to be inauspicious for the cultivation. In the past the Tripuras like other tribes of Tripura enjoyed full freedom and liberty to selects, cut and burn any forest patch for Huk cultivation. But at present, liberty of selection of Huk field is very much restricted by the Forest Department.

When they choose the place, they practiced some religious rites at the selected Huk. At the lower part of the slope land of the selected Huk, by planting three bamboos in the ground. Generally, the bamboo pieces are planted in a horizontal row at the distance of 10th to 12th inches from another. They keep one each Hadul on the top of the bamboo planted. These bamboos represent the Goddess of the Huk. After that the owner of the Huk keep in his hand two pieces of *uakhalak* and toss to look the Goddess of the Huk is agreed with his decision or not. He then drops down the *uakhalak* in the ground with chanting some mantra. It is believed, if one half of the *uakhalak* split falls on the ground adversely and another half reversely, the site is considered to be a suitable for Huk cultivation. But if both halves of the uakhalak fall adversely or reversely, the site would be considered unsuitable. This throwing practice is perform thrice continuously, if they did not show auspicious sign by once. But the auspicious sign as indicated above are not obtained, the site is considered abandoned. Then they left that particular field and search for another new place. They observe religious rite Lampra Uathob in the selected place for Huk.

In the second stage the selected site forest is cutting by male members of the family cutting of Huk is a start from the middle month of December-March. Although the little boys and girls ranging from ten to fifteen years in a family all are engaged their specific duty in the Huk. But the cutting of the *bolong* (forest) is mainly done by the male members and the woman folk help them. The cutting forest of bamboos and plants are left spreading some days for drying. Before cutting they observe religious rite Lampra Uathob in the selected place for Huk.

Tools and implements required for Huk operation were: Dasukai, Dama, Dasha, Chekhara (are kinds of chopper and digger), Ruwa (àxe), Chempai, Kalbang and Maikhok. Dama, Dasa and Ruwa are used for cutting forest which is full of bushes and cleaning of the Huk. By dasukai they dig for sowing seeds and at the same time they carrying seeds in the Champai to be sown. Kalbang and Maikhok are used during harvesting.

At the third stage, when it become dry they set fire to the fell trees and branches of the Huk and burnt as Huk sok-w. It is to be noted that setting of fire should be done before the rains; otherwise it will be wet and will not burn well. It is the plants and bushes which are left to be sundries for several days after cutting; it should not less than twenty to twenty-five days. More over it is done when they are satisfied that every thing has dried up well and there is wind to help. The burning bushes are required two to three days for cooling down. The Huk would yield higher production and it will be less laborious if the whole Huk is burnt into ashes without leaving any thing unburnt. The ashes are considered to be good manure for the fertilization of the soil. It is promoted good production, for that the burnt ashes are evenly distributed over the entire field and levelled up. The unburnt and half burnt roots and trees are cut down and removed from the Huk land.

Sometimes, the production of the Huk also depends on this clearance of the unburnt materials from the Huk. But the clearance of the unburnt materials from the Huk is very difficult job. Usually the big trees are not cut to the root; they left up certain height so that creepers can not climb up them. After that they make a Banok with bamboo and thatch. The Banok is build to take rest and have their lunch. This operation is completed by the month of March-April.

Then in the next stages, they sow seeds of paddy, jute, cotton, chillies, vegetable seeds, Sesame, maize, and different types of cucumber are sown together on the same land. The sowing is generally done in the month of April-May after the first rain. In the sowing work, they use Dasukai instead of plough for digging holes. They are sowing seeds, digging soil with the left hand by Dasukai and pouring seeds in the holes with right hand taking from the Chempai which is placed at the left waist. All the members of the family take part in it. They start digging and sowing from the top of the hill and then gradually come to bottom of the hill in a line. After completing the first line they climb up the hill and again starts digging and sowing. This process continues till the sowing operation is completed. The crops which are sown by digging holes are paddy, cotton, Thabochok, etc. There are some seeds which they sprinkle around the field.

At the sixth stage, Huk tang-w literally means performance of weeding in the Huk. The weeding is basically done thrice in a season as Hatalni, Kacharni pala and Aduk ramani. Thrice weeding is done as an interval of one month or so, normally in the month of June, July and August. It is depending on the strength of short wild grass and creepers numbers of growth and cover in the Huk, which is known as Sam. Weeding is done for the healthy growth of the plants and well crops. Primarily weeding is done with hand and Daborok whereas in some case they used Dasukai. Weeding and undesirable sprouts are uprooted and the base of the each plant is cleared from its full growth. All the family member woman and children are engaged in the cleaning. But the cleaning is done depending on the growth of unwanted plants. After the weeding plants are allowed to grow and bear fruits.

In the seventh stage, they constructed a Gayreng for watching crops and harvesting, like all other tribe of Tripura. They do not keep unwatched and unprotected their Huk cultivation, although it stands at a certain distance from their residence. It is made in order to keep keen watch over the wild animals with a view to scaring them away. To keep safeguard the bearer fruits in the Huk from wild animals such as hill rats, different kinds of birds, monkeys, deer, elephants and especially boars. Soon after fruits become mature, all animals and birds rush for falls and entering in the Huk. During this period they are very much alert and keep constant watch over the Huk. They drive out as much as possible all animals and birds approaching in the field.

The Gayreng is build ten to twelve feet in high from the ground. It is made by bamboo and thatched roof. The Gayreng roof is slopes down on two sides and it has fencing with Bera. The platform is made of bamboo and its engsai. There is a ladder or steps made of bamboo or wood to climb up to the platform. The sizes of the Gayreng are generally 15 ft. x 9ft. in its measurement. During the Huk season whole family shifted to the Gayreng and they also carry their livestock along with them.

The common enemies of the Huk crops of animals are uak bolong (wild boar), Mayung (elephants), Makhara (monkeys), Mufur and birds like Batho, Tokcher, Tokthu, piyara, etc. To drive out the birds and animals they prepared peculiar sound by bamboo. The sound which produced from bamboo is prepared as, bamboo poles with the upper portion of each splinted into four parts are vertically planted all around the field, and a long rope is tied to all these splinted parts. When the watcher of the field pulls the rope, it produced a peculiar sound by the clapping of the bamboo poles, which help to drive out the animals and birds. Besides, they make fire in the night to protection from wild animals and also used traps to catch animals. All these are the few means and methods of drive out animals and birds used by the Huk cultivators and protected their fields.

In the final stage, they harvest paddy as *mai ra-w* and then *Nara-mog-w.* After harvesting paddy, they collect cotton, sipling, cuts Mesta, etc. In the Huk cultivation varieties of vegetables and paddy are produced as cited above. It is all harvested stage by stage in different times depending on maturity, ripe and becomes ready for harvesting. Huk cultivation is harvested particularly from June and it ended by the month of October. During the harvesting both man and woman of the family engaged in the field. In this time they used Kabang to collect the paddy and Chekhara for *mai rani* (paddy cut). The kalbang is carried at the back, hanging by fastening it with string called Lamak Buduk around the head. After cutting paddy they pour in the kalbang and gather at a particular place. Harvesting is depending upon the maturity for different yields in different months. Fruits like Thaichumu (cucumis), Mongphol (Melon), Daramai and Sasha (cucumber), Lokbanda, Bakhur, Khumsaini, Amachang, Muicheng, Banda, Moka (maize), etc., are harvested at the beginning in the month of June. The *Maising-a* (a type of corn), *Khakluk* (white gourd), *Swmwrwi* (Pumpkin), *Muilog* (bottle gourd), Sapai (long bean), phandok (brinjal), etc. are harvested in the month of July. This seasonal fruits and vegetables are brought into the market for sell. It helps them economically to purchase other things which they can not produce.

The types of Mai (paddy) sown in the Huk are Gelong, Beddi, Bathiya, Kokpra, Ausha, Sailogma, Tippra chinal, Nathaig and Maimil like watalok, Mwsui, Rampoddama. Mesta (jute), Sipling (sesamum), Khool (cotton), Silik (Turmeric), Haicheng (ginger), etc. are harvested during the period from August to October. At the last they harvested types of ground potatoes like sammuwa-tha, Thamuichu and Thaklog, Thamaitwk, Thaplam, Tharajung, Thaktwi, Thabarchak, Gorasi, Thatoktwi, Thabokhokkachak. Harvested paddy brought at the one placed and kept heaps for threshing. The threshing of paddy is known as Mai Nakmani. Mai Nakmani is a process, both man and woman threshing with legs continuously till corns are separated from its plants. After threshing, it is winnowing by Baileng as Mai chok-w or Mai sib-w. Then it is stored in the Mai Nok or Rabang. It is help them to manage whole years, if is find extra they used to sell it in the market. In case mesta, after cutting, it is kept fifteen to twenty-five days under the water to be rotten. Then the rotten skin of Mesta are taken out and kept in the sun for dry.

The sipling are threshing by beating with a wooden or bamboo rod, which is in Tripura language called as *Sipling Bumani*. Here also same as Mai Nakmani, they beat continuously until and unless the corns are separated from the plants. It is also winnowed with bailing. The dry mesta skin and Sipling are sold in the market for economic assistant. From the Khul they prepared threads by chwrkhi, as Khul Lubmani, with that, cloths are woven for their daily use with different design.

Huk cultivation at present creates acute problems by causing severe soil erosion. More over the yield of crop raised through Huk cultivation is not high and can not sustain the cultivators for the whole years. The yield from Huk is very low in comparison to other forms of cultivation. Another point is that due to expansion of plantation works in the forest areas by the Rubber planter and forest Department, land for Huk becoming scarce. So, mind of the people turned from Huk to plough cultivation and to Rubber plantation rapidly.

Plough Cultivation or Wetland Cultivation

Plough cultivation is done in the low land. Scarcity of Huk cultivation, lead people to observed plough cultivation and shifting to permanent cultivation as well as settlement. The plough cultivation is much more better then the Huk cultivation in the production as well as income. Plough cultivation in the low land is permanent, continuously can cultivate varieties of paddy, vegetables, cucumbers, potato, onion, sugarcane, etc seasonally in the whole years. It is not like Huk that after one or two years you need to shift, you can cultivate continuously year after year in case of low land cultivation which in Tripura language is known as Pathor.

To cultivate Pathor, first of all soil is needed to wet fully. The land is ploughed by cow and buffaloes, but at present they started to use machinery and its technique. Here they sowed paddy seedlings. In the plough cultivation weeding is done twice to the unwanted plants in between the paddy plants. After that all performance are same as Huk cultivation like threshing, winnowing and storing.

The agricultural implements used by the Tripuras Wetland cultivations are :

Gada (The plough).	Jual (The yoke).
Hapta (The leveller).	Kodal (The hoe).
Chekhara (The sickle).	Ura (The basket).
Dasa (The scythe).	Ruwa (The axe).
Daborok (A kind of scythe).	

Recently, they started turning again in the slopes land, but this time not for shifting cultivation, but for permanent cultivation that is Rubber plantation, coconut, tea, etc. Plantations which are giving satisfactory economics support to the family.

Vegetables Cultivation

Tripuras cultivate different types of vegetable for their daily uses. They are phandok (brinjal), mwilog (bottle gourd), sapai (long bean), ko-keleng (winter bean), khakluk(white gourd), swmrwi (pumpkin), mwiphrai, batima, gorasi, mwitu, gurukuchu, mwlai (radish), hoiro (mustard), thaktwi (sweet potato), phandok Mwkhwrwi (tomato), hongrai, kangla (bitter gourd), thama, aloo (potato), thaichumu, sosha (cucumber), khira, mwirimeal(lady's finger), haicheng (ginger), silik (turmeric), ging^a, phoro, kwitha, mwsu (chilly), bakhwr, etc.

Animal Husbandry

Although huk and wetland cultivation is the principal source of livelihood for majority of Tribal population of Tripura but due to decline production and ill effect of primitive agriculture, large number of Tribal as well as Tripura tribe huk and wetland cultivators are living much below the poverty line. Animal husbandry is also a factor of economic settlement of Tripura tribe. During my field works We have found most of the Tripura families observed as alternative source of occupation on Animal rearing farming. In practical We observed that Tripuras are habituated to rear domestic animals like pig, goat, cattle, local poultry etc. in the home. Rearing of these domestic animals and birds' especially indigenous breed in small number is a tradition of Tribal life and is a part of socio-cultural heritage. In addition these domestic animals and birds provide them a steady source of supplementary income. The tribals are in-general not in the habit of taking milk but they are very much interested to consume meet of pig and poultry. The goats, Pig, poultry birds, etc. are also necessary to offer to their god and goddess to perform social custom and rites.

Piggery

Pig rearing is a popular activity among the Tripuras but here above 90% breeds are local. The local breeds are small in size, yield less meat and take much time to attain marketability. So for economic settlement of Tripuras improved breeds may be utilized to upgrade local pig by cross breeding which are acceptable to the tribal people and meat also fetches remunerative market rate. The new born piglets will be reared and then sold of in the market for meat purpose which will be ensured higher economic return to the Tripuras families.

Goatery

It is also observed that a vast area of Tripuras inhabited is under waste and hill lands covered thickly with vegetation where rearing of goat may be taken up by the Tripuras. Rearing of goats in such Tripuras area is practically no cost involved in their maintenance. In the local and urban markets of Tripura is very good demand for mutton. The goats can be easily maintained on grazing and browsing with minimum cost and Tripuras will be able to get maximum profit.

Local Poultry

Local poultry rearing in the home is very familiar among Tripuras. It is also a profitable if a scientific management practice is adopted. Poultry birds can supply egg and meat. So there is great scope for economic settlement of Tripuras. In this connection it is a suggestion to improve the local breed of poultry birds through crossing with exotic improved breed for further distribution of cross poultry birds to the common Tripuras poultry growers.

Economics Support from Food-Gathering Activities

Food gathering activities of Tripuras mainly consists of collection of roots, fruits, tubers, flowers, etc from near by hillock or Bolong (forest). These types of food collection are mainly done by woman, the male members hardly co-operate them. It is sold near by market by the collectors and earned some money in exchange. Wild edible products collected by tribals of Tripura have been categorised as :

A. *Edible shoots and stems tubers:* These are Mwiua (Bamboo shoot), Tharai *(Alpinia allughas Rose),* Bring (Alpinia), Gandari *(Alocassia odora Roxb),* Batima *(Amorphophallus companulatus Roxb),* Muitu (arum), etc.

B. *Roots and Tubers :* Thaborchok *(Dioscorea glabra),* Thakun, Thabalai kiting, Phaunma, etc.

C. *Leafy Vegetable :* Kenchiri *(Monochoria hastate L),* Kantha *(Lasia spinosa L),* Muitalbi, Aorai, Sakamu-baklab *(Centella asiatica),* Samborma *(Boerhavia diffusa),* Gonga basog, Muikun-chak *(Diplazium polypodiodes),* Mwicheng, bakhwr, Mwigilee, etc.

D. *Flowers :* Mui-khun *(Musa acuminate colla),* Muitu bobar, etc.

E. Fruits: Khamkha *(Solanum torvum Swartz),* Duspe, Tokha Thaichumu *(Coccinia grandis),* Baikang *(canavalia gladiata jacq),* Owakere *(parkia javanica lamk),* Charam bathai, Jam, Kak *(Garcinia cowa Roxb)*, Kusumai *(baccaurea ramiflora lour)*, Thaicherem, Thaimachak, Thaitoi, balong boroi, Thaichuk bolong, etc.

F. Mushroom: Tribals of Tripura are very fond of mushroom which they collect from the forest. They are Buphang-mui-khu-mu (Clitocybe), Mwikhu-mu-rathoi, Mwikhu-mu-hapalak, chakab-mui-khumu, etc.

Hunting

The male Tripuras goes for hunting animals and birds in the forest and hills. Strenuous activities which is not possible with woman is co-operated by man. Beside that, they also collected fire wood. It is for house as well as for selling. Of course, it is practised by all other tribes of the North-East.

Hunting animals and birds is an important food gathering in the Tripura society. Almost all animals and birds are hunted for food, except some flesh eating animals and birds like Tiger, crow, Muphur, etc. Hunting activities is practised from childhood. Of course, they do not hunt always for food purpose but they hunt some time to protect their crops and themselves. The elders teach and impart training to the youngsters regarding the use of weapons and traps during the hunting operation.

Some methods and techniques of hunting used by Tripuras are:

Khwi (Spear Trap)

Depending on the animals intended to be killed, a long bamboo tied to a few sticks is placed one and a half feet to three feet above the ground parallel to the track frequented by the wild animals. The anterior part of the bamboo is forcibly bent back with ropes and sticks. A small and sharp spear made of dry bamboo is tied to the anterior end of the bamboo. The string is extended across the track and is the main controlling factor of the bent bamboo. When an animal passes through the track it touches the string and disturbs the pole and releases it which at once strikes the animal with its spear. If the animal is accurately speared, it may even die on the spot. Wild boars, deers, tigers, and bears are killed with the help of this popular deadly trap called 'Khwi'.

Hakor (Pit Fall)

Pit fall is mainly used for killing ferocious animals like tiger. A deep and circular pit serves the purpose. The pit has to be deep enough so that the animal might not be able to make its way out. The pit is covered with leaves and twigs to give it a natural show. Bait is placed in the middle of the pit. When the animal comes for the bait, it falls instantly and gets itself imprisoned in the deep pit.

Batul (Bow or Pellet)

The Tripuras use arrows as well as bows largely in the hunting operation. A bow is strong bamboo spilt curved with a strong rope. In the mid point of the string a well knitted half dome shape curve measuring 75" x 90" approximately is make in between the main string. The string is sufficiently pulled; the earthen pellet kept inside it is grasped and released along with the string to hit the object aimed at. Expert can hit a small bird from a distance of 100 meters.

Nill (Type of Gum to Trap Birds)

Bird lime is an adhesive prepared out of sticky juice of jack fruit and banyan tree. The lime is applied on sticks which are planted around bait. Once the bird is caught, it tries to free itself by fluttering, but the more it flutters the more it gets stuck.

Fishing

Another important food collection is a fishing which prevails so widely among all section of the Tribal. Fishing is open to both sexes. Fishing is done individually as well as collectively throughout the year, and every family has basic fishing appliances. Some of the important means and methods of catching fishes as adopted by the Tripuras are as discussed below :

Scooping

In the winter season when the water recedes, a group of people go to the river and make bunds across the river. From the compartment the water is scooped out to the other side with the help of 'mairang' and 'Pokai' an implement. Fishes are caught when almost all the water has been scooped out.

Yakbai Ah Rwm-mani (Bare Hand Fishing)

This simplest and oldest method of catching fish by bare hand is still a common practice among the Tripuras, particularly during the winter season when the water starts receding. There are two main methods of bare hand fishing. One of the two methods is capturing the fishes in their holes of hiding in the shallow water. In the other method, a few fishermen violently stir the shallow water and thus stupefy the fishes which start floating due to excessive tiredness. The fishes are equally distributed among the participants.

Duk (Thorn Trap)

This cylindrical thorn-trap woven in a manner to allow water to pass freely is open at one end. A conical structure with thorns at the cone made of the extended sharpened ends of the bamboo splits with which the very structure has been woven is placed at the opening end of the main and cylindrical structure, but the thorns obstruct the coming out of the trapped. A fence is made across the river with an opening in the middle facilitating setting of the trap. The trap is set against the water current during the early monsoon when the fish start moving upward against the stream and the process is downward along with the water current.

Chokhara (A Funnel Shaped Fish Trap Made of Bamboo)

The chokhara is a simple conical trap made of single bamboo piece split into several strips at one end. These strips are then tied to a wild loop. The chokhara is generally placed on a shallow waterbed either in a stream or in an inundated field.

Bwrshing (Fishing Rod Made of Bamboo, Stick, Line and Iron Hook)

Bwrshing is another interesting fishing technique by hook. Iron hooks are procured from the local markets, and earthworms are used as bait.

Sai or Jal (Fishing Net)

It is a catching net with lead beads tied at regular intervals along the periphery; it is used in both shallow and deep water. When an angler casts the net, it is thrown wide open on the water surface, and it instantaneously goes down trapping the fish within its pockets. With a strong rope, the net is dragged ashore.

Household Industry

Handicrafts

Handicrafts are another important economics assistant to the Tripura family. It is evident; Tripura families are traditionally economics self- sufficient and self-contained but industrial revolution and global modernization force them dependable. Self-contained economic pattern prevailing in Tripuras, lead each and every member of a family well-skilled in all sorts of craft-making which is essentially required by them. At the time they need not purchase any tools or other essential articles from any agencies. Before industrial revolution, hunting tools made and used by Tripuras are Bolom, Donu (bow and arrow), Khwi, Duk, etc by stone, bamboo, wood and Buduk. Regarding other traditional handicrafts made by Tripuras for household, food-gathering, storing, and producing of domestic activities like Kalbang, Khangra, Chempai, Ura, Nokhai (are used as carrying articles), Rabang, Maikhok, Mainok, Sunduk (are used as storing), Yam, Patti, champhrak, pira (are for sleeping and sitting), Ding^wl, Racham, Mwsw-wasung, earthen pots (are crushing and making food), Kiship (hand fan), Gada, Hapta, Juwal (are used for plough) and musical instrument like sumul, Madwl, Chongpreng, Dangdu, etc. are made of bamboo, wood, and earth. In general the Tripuras are experts in household industrial works and agricultural implements. Since these articles are used by the communities, there is also a good market for such articles.

Basketry

The basketry making is an interwoven, which is another important factor of socio-economic and socio-religious activities of Tripuras. Without basket the huk cultivation based society is incomplete. Baskets are mainly made of bamboo and cane strips of different patterns, shapes and sizes for the use of fishing, winnowing, food collection, marketing, rituals and worship. Some baskets are made for containing valuable things belongings. Some are for storing paddy and rice. Some are used for collecting things. In a nutshell it may be said that the Tripuras handicraft products are too elaborate in its nature. The skill for making any type of basket is obtained by means of simple visualisation. But the quality or niceties of basket production depends upon the skill of the individual dexterity. Some basket meant for carrying fire-wood and vegetables are made rough and ready matter. But some kinds of baskets for containing valuable things and for going to market place are made nicely and artistically. After all it support economic of the Tripuras families when it is brought to market.

The following are the baskets of the Tripuras.

1. *Kalbang:* It is made of bamboo strips used for carrying articles from one place to another.
2. *Khangra :* It is woven with a gap or hole. It serves the purpose of carrying articles of bigger sizes such as vegetables, roots, fire-wood and utensils etc.
3. *Chempai:* It is also made of bamboo strips smaller then the Kalbang. It is used to carry the paddy seeds and vegetables seeds during huk cultivation and also used to keep different small things.
4. *Khuturuk :* It is used for storing valuable articles.
5. *Dul :* It is a kind of hollow shaped basket used for storing paddy.
6. *Uasung :* It is a bamboo pipe for the purpose of storing dry fish and other spices.
7. *Baileng :* It is very thickly woven, circular and flat tray with a raised rims half inch high. Used for winnowing and drying small quantity of chilli, rice paddy, etc.
8. *Nokhai :* It is also carrying basket closely and artistically woven. It is used for carrying grains, paddy, pulses and also shopping and marketing.
9. *Tokhub :* It is a cage with grotesque and quaint size used for rearing cock.
10. *Lakhub :* It is a kind of rain shield akin almost to a big shell of tortoise made of bamboo strips staffed with dry palm leaf. It protects the head and the back from the rain. The plough man ploughing the field uses lakhub.
11. *Chaileng-ni:* It resembles baileng in shape with only difference in having gaps in between the woven

networks. It is used for cleaning, filtering and separating grains from unwanted stones, sand, etc.

Besides above mentioned bamboo made articles, Tripuras have to make more different kinds of traps for catching fish from the streams and brooks. The following are the traps or tools.

1. *Chokhra* : A funnel shaped fish traps. To the purpose of setting chokhra they build up make-shift barrage covering entire breadth of the streams thereby making several passages for setting chokhra. The fish running down the stream through barrage are caught in the chokhra where from they collect the fish early morning.
2. *Duksa* : It is a barrel-shaped basket of larger size with a trapping device mouth through which fish can easily enter but cannot go out. It is kept submerged in the river water at any place.

Weaving

The art of weaving is playing an important role in the life and economy of the Tripura tribe. It is also well known among the primitive hill tribes of North-east India. It is a purely family-oriented activity, and textiles are woven to meet the requirements of the family members. Every family has a loom to weave the textiles for all family members. It is mostly confined to the woman folk, although they might be busy with the domestic chores.

In the primitive's day, the raw material used in the textile weaving is cotton. Every family procures cotton flowers from its own plantation in the Huk field. Cotton seeds are generally sown in the month of April-May, and its flowers are plucked in the month of November-December. Collected cotton flowers are then spread across the courtyard for sun dry. The dried cotton flowers are separated from its seeds. In the next stage, the cotton flowers are cleaned in a Chwrkhi (wooden gin) with two rollers geared to resolve in opposite directions. The flowers pass through the roller but the seeds are left behind. It is called in *korokborok* as *Khul-phere-w.* After separated the seeds, the cotton flowers are teased with a bamboo bow to make them soft and fluffy. This bow consists of a stave of bamboo with a wide bass and a narrow top. Its string is made out of cane. The cotton flowers are placed in heaps on the ground, the bow is held in the operator's right hand, and the string is flicked on with a piece of bamboo held by the left hand. The teasing makes the flowers become downy and the process continue until the volume of heap is about five times the original volume of flowers. After cleaning, it is rolled in cylindrical stick. The rolls cotton is then put in the spinning wheel.

The spinning wheel used by Tripuras is of a common type known to most tribal people of Tripura. The spinning wheel consists of three parts, viz., the base, the wheel itself, and the spindle. The base of the wheel is generally made of two wooden pieces being rectangular in cross-section and dovetailed at right angles near about the end of two pieces of wood, which are heavy but short in length. At one end of the base, two vertical wooden posts are inserted at one of the heavier pieces, which are connected at the top by a loosely–fitted horizontal wooden bar that is circular in cross-section. Both ends of this horizontal bar protrude beyond the vertical posts, one of which is larger then the other is. The crank for moving the wheel is attached to this end and the wheel rotates on the horizontal bar.

The spindle is generally manufactured by the village blacksmith out of an iron bar, circular in cross-section, and about 25cm. Long 3cm. in diameter with a point end. A cord passing round it links the drum-like wheel and the spindle. The drum is moved with the help of the crank held by the right hand. The thread is tied to the pointed end of the spindle. When it began to spin; the operator touches lightly the free end of the thread with one end of the sausage of cotton which is held by the left hand. At once, the thread catches the loose fibres of the sausage, the left hand of the weaver begins to move upwards, and the soon the yarning is done. The yarn is then wound round the spindle and the process continued until the twisting fully loads the spindle. The yarn then shifted to a simple tool made of bamboo or wood.

In the next stage, comes dyeing, and the colours generally used by Tripuras are red, black and white. These colours are produced from flowers, leaves and herbs. The colour thus prepared, the yarn is first dipped in the rice-gruel and then dried in the sun. After drying in the sun it is dipped again into the liquid colour for two to three hours, and then the coloured bundles of yarns are taken out and again dried in the sun. Of course, dipping in the rice-gruel and dry in the sun of the yarns are still practiced, but colouring yarn are vague now a days, because coloured yarn are available in the markets. So at present the Tripuras are using coloured yarn from the markets.

After dyeing the yarn, the Tripuras woman begins weaving clothes by a kind of loom called Rikhandwi. It comprises of: (i) the Rikhorok consisting of two bamboo-poles, each 5feet high approx., (ii) the Phernai wasa made of horizontal bamboo beams about 3to 4 feet long, (iii) the soro or breast-rod that rest across the weaver's knees lies in between the phernai wasa and Rwnda to controll the Rikhandwi, (iv) Rwnda which is a rounded yarn, (v) the Rachami a flat wooden flank with pointed ends, 30´´x 3´´ measurement, (vi) khandai is a bamboo stick pointed with ends measuring breadth of the Rikhadwi, (vii) the Beseke at the end of rikhandwi where saban bukur is used to tied, (viii) the saban bukur or the back-strap (or belt) made of buffalo-hide tied to each end of the breast-rod and passing behind the weaver, and (ix) Khulum Thela in which yarn is rolled.

In the present content they do not use the primitive types of weaving, which is so long in a process. Development of industrilisation and globalized communication brought ready-mades goods and services door to door. So they get ready-made goods to weave any items near by markets, like threads, suwing machines, etc. Now days, there is availability of ready-made cloths for any age bar. But, the women-folk used to weave traditional dresses at their respective houses till to-day.

Labour System

The labour system is vague in the Tripuras under the following heads:

Baga (Share)

The share system in the Tripura society is called Baga. In this system the owner gives to a person his/her cultivable land for a period. The production crop is divided between the owner and cultivators equally. The land owner gives his land and seeds to the cultivator. No document is executed in this respect. The owner of the land gives his land orally. Not only cultivates land they also gives baga of domestic animals. This system of land sharing is also practised by other tribal of Tripura.

Yaul Khil-laimani (Exchange of Labour):

In this system, one person helps another person in his agricultural or any other types of work and in return the other person also helps this person in its work. No payment is made by either side in this connection. It is a mutual help between one person and another. Here, the party works first called yaul-khilmani and the party that renders its service in return of it is called yaul-sumani.

Gabur (Domestic Servant)

In the Tripura society domestic servant also plays an important role in the agricultural work as well as other domestic works. He is generally appointed for one year and is paid either in cash or on payment of 10 to 15 mond paddy (400 to 550 K.G.) plus his fooding. No female servant is engaged for agricultural works.

Beside above cited system, they work as daily labour, government and semi-government and private institution.

Problems of economics activities in the inhabited area of Tripuras:

The Tripuras are born huk cultivators. Failure of monsoon, infestation of crop pest and disease causes starvation among them. Main problems of economics activities are :

1. They generally grow single crop on the available plain land.
2. Poor irrigation facilities in the Tripuras inhabited area.
3. Due to hilly terrain lands are susceptible to excessive soil erosion, fertility loss within a short period if proper care and management practices are not adopted.
4. Poor facilities of Agricultural technology.
5. Less infrastructural facilities in the hill farm.
6. Poor transport communication and marketing.
7. Poor capital investment due to economic backwardness of Tripuras cultivators.
8. Fragmented land holding.
9. Lack of adequate credit from bank.
10. Lack of education.
11. Lack of proper training.
12. Lack of proper guidance in the economics activities.
13. No use of high yielding variety of crops.

Suggestion

Economic settlement, education and development are necessary in day to day life of the Tripura tribe. Economic settlement of Tripuras it is felt essential to provide the suitable land, permanent house and proper education, simultaneously it is suggested to utilise the top of the high hills and step slopes permanently for forest plantation. The gentle slopes are to be utilized for growing different crops like upland paddy, huk paddy, sesame, cotton, jute, maize, green gram, red gram, black gram, cow pea, sugarcane, chilly, huk cucurbits, etc. arranging in descending order to their moisture requirement and soil type. In plane hillock land ginger, turmeric, sweet potato, groundnut, thabochok, etc. may be grown. In the low land with assured irrigation facilities high yielding or hybrid paddy, vegetables like potato, cabbage, cauliflower, radish, bean, bitter gourd, etc. may be cultivated with good quality seeds, application of manures and fertilizer and integrated pest management practices followed until they are not leaving primitive huk cultivation.

For the improvement of huk cultivation they may practice:

1. Construction of fire line around huk plots.
2. Replacement of old traditional varieties by the improved varieties.
3. Use of manures and fertilizers to maintain soil fertility.
4. Seed treatment and adoption of integrated pest and disease management technology.
5. Placing different crops in scientific manner for better production and utilization of land.
6. Sowing crops in line across the slopes to conserve soil and moisture.

5

Tripura Tribe and Its Modernization with Reference to Globalization

The Tripura tribe does not live in isolation, economically, politically and socially they are in contact with many other tribal and non-tribal communities of Tripura. The closeness of the Tripuras with other neighbouring communities has altered and is constantly altering their traditional ways of life in all respects. Their present style of living is far deviated from their traditional and customary ways and represents an admixture of tradition and modernity now. The important factors responsible for these changes are:-

i) Economic conditions

ii) Environments

iii) Global urbanization

iv) Education

v) Political situations and

vi) Psychological make up

Economic Factors

The economic factors may be considered as one of the most important factors in changing the traditional pattern of their life. Their traditional pattern of economy has rapidly undergone a transformation. In the past, shifting cultivation played an important role in bringing self-sufficiency to a huk cultivator's family. There was enough virgin land available for huk cultivation. There was no daily market nearby. They did not purchase cotton, jute, rice, firewood, fish, vegetables, etc. from the market. Their chief marketing commodity was salt, kerosene oil and dry fish. The man-land ratio was quite comfortable.

But the situation altered rapidly due to independence when thousand and thousand of Hindu Bangali refugees of Bangladesh erstwhile East Pakistan entered Tripura and entering every day. The refugees out-numbered the Tripuras in some areas. The ratio of the land-people now showed a distinct change. There were too many people and too little land. This affected the self sufficiency of their economy and gradually shrunken additional source of income. They then began to work as daily labourer in the forest Department, P.W.D. etc.

In the past, the reciprocal labour system existed among the Tripuras. The exchange of the labour for agriculture or house construction work was their traditional system. But now they are very much commercialized. The system of reciprocal labour has been replaced by labour for cash payment.

Government service is now a subsidiary source of income to the educated section of the Tripuras. The younger generation is very much attracted by the government service which is regarded as a boost to their social status. Government employees who own agricultural land in addition are held in high esteem. Many of them are busy in extending their property and providing better education for their children. The economic disparity has been growing bigger and bigger within their community day by day. Thus, the emergence of landholding and landless classes in the traditionally classless Tripura community may now be described as a new dimension to their economic life.

With the development of communication, markets, and business centers have come up in their localities. Many of them purchase their essential commodities from these markets. Many small traders often come to these villages to purchase agricultural products and take them to urban centers. This has produced a number of go-getters in the community who are aware of the current market prices of each and every agricultural commodity.

The involvement of the Tripuras in the trade and commerce was almost zero even a few years ago. They were completely dependent on agriculture. But now they are gradually taking up this line of profession. Now Tripuras, though few in number are engaged and giving interest in the business of dry fish, grocery, stationary, timber, transport, fishery, etc.

The globalized economic organizations like insurance, large scale multi-purpose co-operative societies, Banks and agents of various so called investment companies have now been successful to a great extent in changing their age-old custom of borrowing from local money lenders under heavy interest.

The extension of the facility of the cattle insurance scheme has saved them from the danger of any sudden death amidst their bullocks, cows,etc. Now they don't need to go to the village money lenders to borrow money at an exorbitant rate of interest.

Now, modern cò-operative society branches and small traders are available in all the local markets of the Tripuras inhabitants. They are purchasing directly from the producer. This has helped them to get just price, for their products. The steady growth of the number of Tripuras share-holders in these co-operatives indicates their popularity. These modern co-operative societies are gradually replacing their indigenous traditional co-operatives.

The banks are also playing an important role in changing their traditional economic system. The Tripuras are now aware of rules and regulation of bank loans. Many of them have transaction with banks.

Though even to-day, the Tripuras are following the traditional method of cultivation, their gradual awareness regarding the utility of manure, insecticides, hybrid seeds, irrigation facilities undoubtedly show the trends of globalization.

In this way, the Tripuras got mixed up with numerous urban characteristics which have greatly affected the homogeneous and traditional ways of life.

Environmental Factors

The early Tripura hamlets were surrounded by hills, small hillocks and forests. They produced various kinds of agricultural products, hunted wild animals and collected firewood, sheets of bamboos and roots of various kinds of herbs and creepers which were used in the preparation of food item.

But globalisation, urbanisation, deforestation and the growth of population have changed the ecological balance and also their traditional ways of life. The forests which meant so much to them at one time are now no longer all that precious. They now have to purchase bamboo, thatch, tree, etc. for the construction of their houses, which was unthinkable to them even forty years ago. The Tripuras folk song, folk literature, folk administrative and folk festivals which developed and flourished around the forest and huk cultivating has been gradually disappearing due to the extinction of huk cultivation.

Impact of Global Education

With the spread of global education many Tripuras prefer residing in school and college hostels in Tripura as well as other places. As a result of this contact with the outside world they are becoming aware of the customs and traditions of other communities tribal and non-tribal. Consequently their outlook, attitude, etc. have undergone quite a remarkable change. This change is reflected in their words, actions, modes of behaviour etc.

Owing to their stay in hostels, far away from home in early childhood they have little scope to get acquainted with their own traditions and customs. Moreover owing to the influence of urban life, they fail to form any high opinion about their own culture and traditions. This attitude of the young generation is gradually weakening the age-old socio-religious beliefs of the Tripura.

In the past, the folk song was very popular among the Tripuras. The Naitong rachabmung, Porunda Tanmani and Anok rachabmung with historical themes and jokes were very much popular among them. But now-a-days all those Naitong and Anok rachabmung, jokes, etc. are towards extinction on their way. Their traditional songs are now sung to the tunes of popular Hindi and Bengali films songs.

Similarly, folk riddles, proverbs and folk tales are liked only by females and elder personalities of their community. The young generation is completely indifferent.

The Impact of Politics

The Tripuras are still well-known for their unity. In the past the power and authority enjoyed by the chief of their Naran is unparalleled. He holds an unquestionable command over the members of his community in the state level. In the village the Ruwaja holds supreme powers and authorities.

But since independence, the various elections of parliament, state legislature and village panchayet have created a new awareness among them in the matter of political rights and privileges.

All India Political parties like congress, C.P.I. (M) and regional parties like T.U.J.S, I.P.F.T., I.N.P.T, N.C.P., etc. have followers in them. With the emergence of diverse political parties with different political ideologies- the once united Tripuras are now politically divided. All these various groups are now guided by their respective political party leaders and not by their traditional chief.

Now-a-days, possession of western education, secular outlook, sound economic condition and oratory capability are receiving more importance than the age-old leadership of the village councils.

There is a change in the values, too. The old and experienced village leaders are gradually fading out of the limelight due to the newly emerged concept of political leadership. The young generation more than make up for any gap created by the non-participation of the older generation in the present political activities.

The change that occurred in the economic, social, political and environmental condition of the Tripuras have left distinct mark on their food habits, dresses and ornaments, games and sports, their attitude towards traditional system of treatment of any illness etc.

Food Habits

The use of spices and other modern devices is gradually replacing the old ways of preparation of the food by boiling, grilling roasting over an open fire etc. Many of them now relish non-traditional food items as a result of living in boarding houses.

The gradual deforestation has also changed their food habit to some extent. Their traditional cakes Awan are not as popular as sweets available in shops now. In the past they used to take it during cold, wet mornings, sitting around a fire and warming their shivering bodies at the same time. But it is a rare sight now-a-days.

The change that has come over their dresses, ornaments and also style of sporting them is also significant. Tailor made shirts and trousers have replaced kamchilik borok, tenja and rematwi. In the past, the Tripura women used to wear risa with splendor designed to cover their breast and rinai at the lower part of body but at present it has been replaced by tailor made bra and salwar. Their traditional ornaments have been replaced by glass and fibres bangle, city gold and imitation jewellers, earrings, necklaces etc. from the local market.

In the past, their necessary clothes were woven on their traditional handlooms. The yarns of the clothes were spun from the cotton collected from their huk. But in the modern market system has replaced it by colourful ready-made yarns.

In respect of house-hold articles, there are seen lost of change. Modern suitcase, cup and saucer, various kinds of aluminium, steel and melamine's utensils, buckets, etc. have replaced their traditional bamboo and earthenware articles and utensils.

Their traditional games and sports like Sukui thwngmani, Tokla Tanlaimani, Dul-laimani, Achukwi phran-Swlaimani etc. have been replaced by foot-ball, valley ball, cricket, carrom, chest, etc. The mode of recreation has also changed. The folk games and sports of the Tripuras are on their way out.

The traditional system of treatment by the ochai is losing its popularity day by day. They no longer depend completely on the magical formulae of the ochai for their treatment. The villagers now want immediate result. Unlike the older generation, they have no time and patient to wait and see.

The expansion of modern medical facilities in the tribal areas, the availability of medicines for certain common diseases like malaria, dysentery, etc. in the nearby medical stores, and the immediate result of these patent medicines are the important factors for this change in attitude of Tripuras.

The negligent attitude of the modern doctors and the educated section of Tripuras towards their traditional system of treatment are discouraging the youth generation to learn this profession.

But still to-day, the traditional system is popular among the women folk. A good number of tradition-oriented Tripuras, however, take the story of the efficacy of the ochai is treatment with a pinch of salt. In the present adverse economic situation, it has become very difficult on the part of traditional ochai to survive due to the hard competition on the part of modern allopathic medical practitioner.

Post-Globalization of Cultural Dynamics

The culture which ceases to be dynamic becomes a burden to its people. The Tripura culture is a dynamic and it has been enriched by the influence of different tribal and non-tribal culture from time immemorial.

It is to be noted that the Tripuras culture is based mainly on their different socio-religious functions which include the rites, rituals, ceremonies, worships, customs, manner, beliefs and the folk literature connected with them. So, in discussing the influence of other culture, cultural contact, conflict and acculturation in Tripura tribe attention should be paid to the above socio-religious institutions and functions.

Bibliography

1. B.C. Allen, *Tripperah in Census of India 1901*.
2. B.C. Allen, E.A. Gait, G.G.H. Allen, *Gazetteer of Bengal and North East India,* H.F. Howand.
3. S.B.K. Debbarma, *The tribes of Tripura: A Dissertation,* Directorate of Research, Department of Tribal Welfare for SC& ST, Govt. of Tripura; Agartala: 1971.
4. R.K. Acharyya, *The Murasings,* Directorate of Research, Department of Tribal Welfare for SC& ST, Govt. of Tripura; Agartala: 1999.
5. Chandramani Debbarma, *Glory of Tripura Civilization*.
6. Priyabrata Bhattacharjee, *Tribal Pujas and Festivals of Tripura,* Directorate of Research, Department of Tribal Welfare for SC& ST, Govt. of Tripura; Agartala: 1994.
7. Dr. Dwijendra Lal Bhomik, *Tribal Religion & Tripura,* Tribal Research Institute, Govt. of Tripura; Agartala: 2003.

8. Raida : *Tripura Chubalai Buthu* (beg.).

9. *Tui : A Quaterly Research Journal on Tribal Life and Culture,* Vol. XII (1st Issue) 2003, Vol. XII (1st, 2nd and 3rd Issue) 2004.

10. A.C. Bhattachariyya, *Progressive Tripura,* Inter-India Publications; New Delhi.

11. Prodeep Nath Bhattacharyee, *The Janmatiyas of Tripura,* Directorate of Research, Govt. of Tripura; Agartala: 1983.

12. Jagadis-Gan Chaudhury, *Tripura: the Land and Its People,* Leeladevi Publication; New Delhi:1980.

13. Dr. J. Ganchoudhury, *The Reangs of Tripura,* Directorate of Research, Department of Tribal Welfare for SC& ST, Govt. of Tripura; Agartala: 1983.

14. Debapriya Debbarma, *Treatise on Traditional Social Institutions of the Tripura community,* Directorate of Research, Department of Tribal Welfare for SC& ST, Govt. of Tripura; Agartala: 1983.

15. Sukhendu Debbarma, *Origin and Growth of Christianity in Tripura.*

16. Omesh Saigal, *Tripura,* Concept Publishing Company; Delhi: 1986.

17. P.C. Muanthanga, *The Harvest Field of Tripura,* Carey Research & Communication center, NEIMBCC; Shillong: 1998.

18. R.G Singh & A. D'barma, *History of Tripura,* Tripura State Tribal Cultural Research Institute & Museum, Govt. of Tripura; Agartala: .1997.

19. Dr. S.B. Saha, *Socio-economic Survey of the Noatia Tribe,* Directorate of Research, Department of Tribal Welfare for SC& ST, Govt. of Tripura; Agartala: 1980.

20. Sir H. Risley, *The People of India.*

21. Letthuama Darlong, *The Darlongs of Tripura*, Tribal Research Institute, Govt. of Tripura; Agartala: 1995.
22. R.H. Sneyd Hutchinson, *Chittagong Hill Tracts.*
23. A.K. Poul, *Tripura Small But Beautiful.*
24. Dr. Bibhuti Bhushan Sarkar. *Economic Settlement of Tribal Youths in Tripura*, Tribal Research Institute, Govt. of Tripura; Agartala: 2007.
25. Dr. Narendra Chandra Nath. *Sri Rajmala*, Tribal Research Institute, Govt. of Tripura; Agartala:1999.
26. Bibhas Kanti Kilikdar, *Tripura of Eighteenth Century with Samsher Gazi Against Feudalism (A historical Study)*, Tripura State Tribal Cultural Research Institute & Museum, Govt. of Tripura, 1995.
27. Dr. Suchintya Bhattacharya. *The Halams of Tripura: From Primitive to Modernity*, 2003.
28. Suren Debarma, *A Short Account of Tripuri Society*, 2006.
29. Dr. Suchintya Bhattacharya, *The Kaipengs*, Tribal Research Institute, Govt. of Tripura; Agartala: 1980.
30. Paushali Das, *Wild Edible Plants of Tripura Tribes*, Tripura State Tribal Cultural Research Institute & Museum, Govt. of Tripura, 1997.
31. Dr. Suchintya Bhattacharya, *From Jhuming to Tapping*, Directorate of Research, Department of Tribal Welfare for SC& ST, Govt. of Tripura; Agartala: 1992.
32. R.G. Rasak, *History of North Eastern India.*
33. Durgadas Basu, *Shorter Constitution of India.*
34. D.J. Dey, *The Constitution of India* (vol. I to II).
35. J.N. Das, *A Study of Administration of Justice among the Tribes and Races of North Eastern Region.*
36. B.K. Kilikdar, *Customary Laws and Practices of Tripuras of Tripura.*

37. T.H. Lewin, *The Hill Tracts of Chittagong and the Dwellers therein,*

38. Mackenzie, Alexander, *The North East Frontier of India.*

39. Mackenzie, Alexander, *History of the Relations of the Govt. with the Hill Tribes of the North East Frontier of Bengal.*

40. Tripur Chandra Sen, *Tripura in Transition.*

41. Kailash Chandra Singha, *Rajmala* (Vol. I to IV)

42. Kali Prasanna Sen, *Rajmala.*

43. Sandys, E.F., *History of Tripura.*

44. Dr. C.B. Majumder, *Democratic Heritage of Tribes of Tripura,* Tribal Research Institute, Govt. of Tripura; Agartala: 2002.

45. Anugata Mani Akhanda, *Marriages System of Tribal Societies of Tripura,* Directorate of Research, Department of Tribal Welfare for SC& ST, Govt. of Tripura; Agartala.

46. Santosh Kumar Chakraborty, *A Study of Tippara Language,* Directorate of Research, Department of Tribal Welfare for SC& ST, Govt. of Tripura; Agartala: 2002.

47. J.G. Cumming, *Survey and Settlement of the Chakla Rosanabad Estate in the Districts of Tripura and Noakhali.*

48. S.N. Majumder, *Marxism and Language Problem in India,* Delhi, 1970.

49. Dr. S.K. Chatterjee, *Origin and Development of Bengali Language.*

Various Acts and Rules

1. *District Census Hand Book of 1951,* Tripura.

2. *Census of India, 1961,* Tripura- Superintendent of Census Operation, Tripura.

3. *Census of India, 1971,* Tripura- Director of Census Operation, Tripura.
4. *Census of India, 1981,* Tripura— Director of Census Operation, Tripura.
5. *Census of India, 1991,* Tripura— Director of Census Operation, Tripura.
6. *Census of India, 2001,* Tripura— Director of Census Operation, Tripura.
7. G.A. Grierson : *Linguistic Survey of India,* Vol-III, part-II pp. 111-113.
8. Somendra Debbarma: *Tripura Census Bibarani, 1931.*